CAMBRIDGE LIBRARY COLLECTION

Books of enduring scholarly value

English Men of Letters

In the 1870s, Macmillan publishers began to issue a series of books called 'English Men of Letters' – biographies of English writers by other English writers. The general editor of the series was the journalist, critic, politician, and supporter (and later biographer) of Gladstone, John Morley (1838–1923). The aim was to provide a short introduction to each subject and his works, but also that the life should illuminate the works, and vice versa. The subjects range chronologically from Chaucer to Thackeray and Dickens, and an important feature of the series is that many of the authors (Henry James on Hawthorne, Ward on Dickens) were discussing writers of the previous generation, and some (Trollope on Thackeray) had even known their subjects personally. The series exemplifies the British approach to literary biography and criticism at the end of the nineteenth century, and also reveals which authors were at that time regarded as canonical.

Bentley

This biography of the English clergyman, scholar and classicist, Richard Bentley (1662–1742) was published in 1882 in the first series of 'English Men of Letters'. Born in West Yorkshire, educated at Wakefield Grammar School and later at St John's College in Cambridge, Bentley became one of the most respected textual critics of his day. Among students of the Greek New Testament, he is remembered as the first person to define a plan for constructing the whole of the text directly from the original documents. Bentley became a prominent and controversial figure during his time as Master of Trinity College, Cambridge. His temper and his contemptuous treatment of his colleagues led to various attempts to secure his removal and embroiled him in controversy and feuding for the next thirty years. Despite all this, Bentley continued his classical research and published books that are studied to this day.

T0370595

Bentley

R. C. JEBB

CAMBRIDGE
UNIVERSITY PRESS

CAMBRIDGE UNIVERSITY PRESS

Cambridge, New York, Melbourne, Madrid, Cape Town,
Singapore, São Paolo, Delhi, Tokyo, Mexico City

Published in the United States of America by Cambridge University Press, New York

www.cambridge.org
Information on this title: www.cambridge.org/9781108010832

© in this compilation Cambridge University Press 2011

This edition first published 1882
This digitally printed version 2011

ISBN 978-1-108-01083-2 Paperback

English Men of Letters

EDITED BY JOHN MORLEY

BENTLEY

BENTLEY

BY

R. C. JEBB, M.A., LL.D. EDIN.,

KNIGHT OF THE ORDER OF THE SAVIOUR,
PROFESSOR OF GREEK IN THE UNIVERSITY OF GLASGOW,
FORMERLY FELLOW OF TRINITY COLLEGE, CAMBRIDGE.

London:

MACMILLAN AND CO

1882

PREFATORY NOTE.

THE following are the principal sources for an estimate of Bentley's life and work :—

1. Life of Bentley, by J. H. Monk, 4to, London, 1830 : 2nd ed., 2 vols. 8vo, 1833.—2. Bentley's Correspondence, ed. C. Wordsworth, 2 vols., Lond. 1842.—3. Bentley's Works, ed. Alex. Dyce, 1836—38. Vols. I and II :—Dissertation on Letters of Phalaris, (1) as published in 1699, (2) as originally printed in Wotton's *Reflections*, 1697. Epistola ad Ioannem Millium. Vol. III :—Boyle Lectures, with Newton's Letters : Sermons : Remarks upon a late Discourse of Free-thinking : Proposals for an edition of the New Testament : Answer to the Remarks of Conyers Middleton.— 4. Bentley's Fragments of Callimachus, in the edition of Graevius, Utrecht, 1697, reprinted in Blomfield's ed., London, 1815.—5. Emendations on Menander and Philemon (1710), reprinted, Cambridge, 1713.—6. Horace, Camb. 1711, 2nd ed., Amsterdam, 1713.—7. Terence, Camb. 1726, 2nd ed., Amsterdam, 1728.—8. Milton's *Paradise Lost*, Lond. 1732.—9. Manilius, Lond. 1739.

Notes by Bentley appeared during his lifetime in the books of other scholars. Since his death, many more have been published from his MSS. These, while varying much in fulness and value, cannot be overlooked in a survey of the field which his studies covered. The subjoined list comprises the greater part of them:—

On Cicero's Tusculan Disputations, in Gaisford's ed., Oxford, 1805.—Hephaestion, in Gaisford's ed., 1810.—Lucretius,

b

in Oxford ed., 1818.—Horace (curae novissimae), in the Cambridge Museum Criticum I. 194—6, ed. T. Kidd.—Ovid, in the Classical Journal, xix. 168, 258, ed. G. Burges.—Lucan, ed. R. Cumberland, Strawberry Hill, 1760.—Silius Italicus, Class. Journ. iii. 381.—L. Annaeus Seneca, ib. xxxvii. 11, ed. T. Kidd.—Nicander, in Museum Criticum, i. 370, 445, ed. J. H. Monk.—Aristophanes, in Classical Journal, xi. 131, 248, xii. 104, 352, xiii. 132, 336, xiv. 130, ed. G. Burges ; and in Museum Criticum, ii. 126, ed. J. H. Monk.—Sophocles, Theocritus, Bion, Moschus, ed. E. Maltby in Morell's Thesaurus, reprinted in Classical Journal, xiii. 244.—Philostratus, in Olearius's edition (1709).—Hierocles, in Needham's edition (1709).—Plautus, in E. A. Sonnenschein's ed. of the Captivi, p. 135, Lond. 1880.—Iliad i. ii, at the end of J. Maehly's memoir of Bentley (1868), from the MS. at Trinity College, Cambridge.—Selected Notes on the Greek Testament (from the MS. at Trin. Coll. Camb.) including those on the Epistle to the Galatians, in *Bentleii Critica Sacra*, ed. A. A. Ellis, Camb. 1862.—A few anecdota from Bentley's MS. notes on Homer (at Trin. Coll., Camb.) are given below, p. 153.

R. Cumberland's *Memoirs* (4to, 1806, 2nd edition in 2 vols. 8vo, 1807) deserve to be consulted independently of Monk's quotations from them. The memoir of Bentley by F. A. Wolf, in his *Litterarische Analekten* (pp. 1—89, Berlin, 1816), has the permanent interest of its authorship and its date. Rud's Diary, so useful for a part of Bentley's college history, was edited with some additional letters by H. R. Luard for the Cambridge Antiquarian Society, 1860. De Quincey's essay—originally a review of Monk—has every charm of his style ; the sometimes whimsical judgments need not be taken too seriously. Hartley Coleridge's comments on Monk's facts may be seen in the short biography of Bentley which he wrote in the *Worthies of Yorkshire and Lancashire* (pp. 65—174). In 'Richard Bentley, eine Biographie' (Leipzig,

1868), Jacob Maehly gives a concise sketch for German readers, on Monk's plan of a continuous chronological narrative, in which notices of the literary works are inserted as they occur.

It is proper to state the points which are distinctive of the present volume:—1. In regard to the external facts of Bentley's life, I have been able to add some traits or illustrations from contemporary or other sources: these are chiefly in chapters I, III, VII, XII.—2. Chapter VI is condensed from some results of studies in the University life of Bentley's time and in the history of Trinity College.—3. The controversy on the Letters of Phalaris has hitherto been most familiar to English readers through De Quincey's essay on Bentley, or the brilliant passage in Macaulay's essay on Temple. Both versions are based on Monk's. The account given here will be found to present some matters under a different light. In such cases the views are those to which I was led by a careful examination of the original sources, and of all the literary evidence which I could find.— 4. The aim has been not more to sketch the facts of Bentley's life than to estimate his work, the character of his powers, and his place in scholarship. Here the fundamental materials are Bentley's writings themselves. To these I have given a comparatively large share of the allotted space. My treatment of them has been independent of any predecessor.

The courtesy of the Master of Trinity afforded me an opportunity of using Bentley's marginal notes on Homer at a time when they would not otherwise have been accessible. Mr Tyrrell, Regius Professor of Greek in the University of Dublin, favoured me with information regarding a manuscript in the Library. Prof. A.

Michaelis, of Strassburg, and Mr J. W. Clark, of Trinity College, Cambridge, kindly lent me some books and tracts relating to Bentley.

My thanks are especially due to Dr Hort, for reading the proof-sheets of chapter X; and to Mr Munro, for reading those of chapters VIII and IX. To both I have owed most valuable suggestions. For others, on many points, I have been indebted to Dr Luard, Registrary of the University of Cambridge; who, with a kindness which I cannot adequately acknowledge, has done me the great favour of reading the whole book during its passage through the press.

THE COLLEGE, GLASGOW,
February, 1882.

ANNALS OF BENTLEY'S LIFE.

	aet.	I. EARLIER PERIOD.—1662—1699.
1662		Jan. 27. Birth.
1672	10	Goes to Wakefield School.
1676	14	Enters St John's Coll., Cambridge.
1680	18	B.A. Degree.
1682	20	Master of Spalding School. Tutor to J. Stillingfleet.
1683	21	M.A. Degree.
1685	23	**James II.**
1689	27	**William and Mary.** Goes with J. Stillingfleet to Oxford.
1690	28	Ordained. Chaplain to Bp Stillingfleet.
1691	29	*Letter to Mill.*
1692	30	*Boyle Lectures.* Prebendary of Worcester. Temple's *Essay.*
1693	31	*Fragments of Callimachus.* Nominated King's Librarian.
1694	32	Appointed, April 12. Wotton's *Reflections.*
1695	33	Chaplain in Ordinary to King.—F.R.S.—Boyle's *Phalaris.*
1696	34	Promotes reparation of Camb. Press.—D.D.
1697	35	First essay on Phalaris in 2nd ed. of Wotton.
1698	36	Jan. '*Boyle against Bentley.*'
1699	37	Mar. '*Bentley against Boyle.*'—Master of Trin. Coll. Camb.

	aet.	II. At Cambridge.—1700—1742.
1700	38	Feb. 1. Installed at Trin.—Vice-Chancellor.
1701	39	Jan. 7. Marriage.—Archdeacon of Ely.
1702	40	**Anne.**
1702–4	40–2	College reforms.—Swift's *Battle of the Books* (**1704**).
1706–8	44–6	Aids L. Küster, T. Hemsterhuys.
1710	48	Feb. 10. Petition from Fellows of Trin. to Bp Moore.
		Menander and Philemon.—Thornhill's portrait of B.
1711	49	Dec. 8. *Horace.*
1713	51	Bp cites B. to Ely House.—*Remarks* in reply to Collins.
1714	52	First Trial at Ely House.—July 31. Bp Moore dies before judgment has been given. Aug. 1. Death of Queen Anne. **George I.**
1715	53	Jacobite Revolt. B.'s *Sermon on Popery.*
1716	54	Petition from Fellows of Trin. to Crown.
1717	55	B. Regius Prof. of Divinity. George I. visits Cambridge.
1718	56	B. arrested. Deprived of Degrees by Senate (Oct. 17).
1719	57	B. makes terms with Miller.
1720	58	*Proposals* for edition of New Testament.
1724	62	Mar. 26. B.'s degrees restored.—Declines see of Bristol.
1725	63	B.'s Latin speech at Commencement.
1726	64	*Terence* published.
1727	65	**George II.** Death of Newton.
1728	66	George II. at Cambridge.—B.'s illness.—Colbatch active.
1729	67	Bp Greene cites B. to appear. Veto by King's Bench.
1730	68	Senate House opened.
1731	69	Fire at Cottonian Library.
1732	70	B.'s edition of *Paradise Lost.* He undertakes Homer.
1733	71	Second Trial at Ely House.
1734	72	April 27. Bp Greene sentences B. to deprivation.
1735–7	73–5	Efforts to procure execution of the judgment.
1738	76	April 22. End of the struggle. B. remains in possession.
1739	77	*Manilius.*
1740	78	Death of Mrs Bentley.
1742	80	March. Pope's enlarged *Dunciad*, with verses on B. June. B. examines for the Craven.—July 14. His death.

Dates of some Principal Works.

1691	29	Letter to Mill.
1692	30	Boyle Lectures.
1693	31	Fragments of Callimachus.
1699	37	Enlarged Dissertation on Phalaris.
1710	48	Emendations on Menander and Philemon.
1711	49	Horace.
1713	51	Remarks on a late Discourse of Free-thinking.
1726	64	Terence.
1732	70	Edition of *Paradise Lost.*
1739	77	Manilius.

CONTENTS.

CHAPTER VII.

CHAPTER VIII.

CHAPTER IX.

CHAPTER X.

CHAPTER XI.

CHAPTER XII.

CHAPTER XIII.

BENTLEY.

CHAPTER I.

EARLY LIFE. THE LETTER TO MILL.

RICHARD BENTLEY was born on January 27, 1662.
A remarkable variety of interest belongs to his life of
eighty years. He is the classical critic whose thoroughly
original genius set a new example of method, and gave a
decisive bent to the subsequent course of scholarship.
Among students of the Greek Testament he is memorable
as the first who defined a plan for constructing the whole
text directly from the oldest documents. His English
style has a place of its own in the transition from the
prose of the seventeenth century to that of the eighteenth.
During forty years he was the most prominent figure of
a great English University at a stirring period. And
everything that he did or wrote bears a vivid impress
of personal character. The character may alternately
attract and repel; it may provoke a feeling in which
indignation is tempered only by a sense of the ludicrous,
or it may irresistibly appeal to our admiration; but at
all moments and in all moods it is signally masterful.

His birthplace was Oulton, a township in the Parish
of Rothwell, near Wakefield, in the West Riding of
Yorkshire. His family were yeomen of the richer class,
who for some generations had held property in the
neighbourhood of Halifax. Bentley's grandfather had
been a captain in the royalist army during the civil
war, and had died while a prisoner in the hands of
the enemy. The Bentleys suffered in fortune for their
attachment to the cavalier party, but Thomas Bentley,
Richard's father, still owned a small estate at Woodles-
ford, a village in the same parish as Oulton.   After
the death of his first wife, Thomas Bentley, then an
elderly man, married in 1661 Sarah, daughter of Richard
Willie, of Oulton, who is described as a stonemason,
but seems to have been rather what would now be called
a builder, and must have been in pretty good circumstances; he is said to have held a major's commission
in the royal army during the troubles.   It was after
him that his daughter's firstborn was called Richard.
Bentley's literary assailants in later years endeavoured
to represent him as a sort of ploughboy who had been
developed into a learned boor; while his amiable and
accomplished grandson, Richard Cumberland, exhibited
a pardonable tendency to overestimate the family claims.
Bentley himself appears to have said nothing on the
subject.

He was taught Latin grammar by his mother.
From a day-school at Methley, a village near Oulton, he
was sent to the Wakefield Grammar School—probably
when he was not more than eleven years old, as he went
to Cambridge at fourteen. Schoolboy life must have
been more cheerful after the Restoration than it had
been before,—to judge from that lively picture in

North's 'Lives' of the school at Bury St Edmund's,
where the master—a staunch royalist—was forced, 'in
the dregs of time,' to observe 'super-hypocritical fastings
and seekings,' and 'walked to Church after his brigade of
boys, there to endure the infliction of divers holders-
forth.' Then the King came to his own again, and this
scholastic martyr had the happy idea of 'publishing his
cavaliership by putting all the boys at his school into red
cloaks;' 'of whom he had near thirty to parade before
him, through that observing town, to church; which
made no vulgar appearance.' The only notice of
Bentley's school-life by himself (so far as I know) is in
Cumberland's *Memoirs*, and is highly characteristic.
'I have had from him at times whilst standing at his
elbow'—says his grandson, who was then a boy about
nine years old—'a complete and entertaining narrative
of his schoolboy days, with the characters of his different
masters very humorously displayed, and the punishments
described which they at times would wrongfully inflict
upon him for seeming to be idle and regardless of his
task,— *When the dunces*, he would say, *could not
discover that I was pondering it in my mind, and fixing
it more firmly in my memory, than if I had been bawling
it out amongst the rest of my schoolfellows.*' However, he
seems to have retained through life a warm regard for
Wakefield School. It had a high reputation. Another
of its pupils, a few years later, was John Potter,—author
of the once popular work on Greek Antiquities, editor of
Lycophron, and afterwards Archbishop of Canterbury.

Bentley was only thirteen when his father died.
His grandfather, Richard Willie, decided that he should
go to the University without much more delay. The
boy had his own way to make; his father's small estate

had been left to a son by the first marriage; and in
those days there was nothing to hinder a precocious lad
from matriculating at fourteen, though the ordinary age
was already seventeen or eighteen. On May 24, 1676,
'Ricardus Bentley de Oulton' was enrolled in the
Admission Book of St John's College. The choice of a
University may have been influenced by the fact that
John Baskervile, the master of Wakefield School, was a
member of Emmanuel College, Cambridge; the choice of
a College, partly by the fact that some scholarships for
natives of Yorkshire had been founded at St John's by
Sir Marmaduke Constable. Bentley, like Isaac Newton
at Trinity, entered as a subsizar, a student who receives
certain allowances. St John's College was just then the
largest in the University, and appears to have been as
efficient as it was distinguished. The only relic of
Bentley's undergraduate life is a copy of English verses
on the Gunpowder Plot. That stirring theme was long
a stock subject for College exercises. Bentley's verses
have the jerky vigour of a youth whose head is full of
classical allusions, and who is bent on making points.
The social life of the University probably did not
engage very much of his time; and it is left to us to
conjecture how much he saw of two Cambridge contemporaries who afterwards wrote against him,—Richard
Johnson, of his own College, and Garth, the poet, of
Peterhouse; or of William Wotton, his firm friend in
later life—that 'juvenile prodigy' who was a boy of
fourteen when Bentley took his degree, and yet already
a Bachelor of Arts.

Nothing is known of Bentley's classical studies
while he was an undergraduate. His own statement,
that some of his views on metrical questions dated from

earliest manhood (*iam ab adolescentia*), is too vague to
prove anything. Monk remarks that there were no
prizes for classics at Cambridge then. It may be observed, however, that there was one very important
prize—the Craven University Scholarship, founded in
1647. But no competition is recorded between 1670,
when Bentley was eight years old, and 1681, the year
after he took his first degree. The studies of the
Cambridge Schools were Logic, Ethics, Natural Philosophy, and Mathematics. Bentley took high honours in
these. His place was nominally sixth in the first class,
but really third, since three of those above him were men
of straw. The Vice-Chancellor and the two Proctors
then possessed the privilege of interpolating one name
each in the list, simply as a compliment, and they
naturally felt that such a compliment was nothing if it
was not courageous. Bentley's degree had no real like-
ness, of course, to that of third Wrangler now ; modern
Mathematics were only beginning, and the other subjects
of the Schools had more weight ; the testing process, too,
was far from thorough.

Bentley never got a Fellowship. In his time,—indeed, until the present century,—there were territorial
restrictions at almost all Colleges. As a native of
Yorkshire, he had been elected to a Constable scholarship,
but the same circumstance excluded him from a greater
prize. When he graduated, two Fellowships at St John's
were already held by Yorkshiremen, and a third representative of the same county was inadmissible. He
was a candidate, indeed, in 1682 ; but as no person not
in Priest's Orders was eligible on that occasion, he must
have gone in merely to show what he could do. The
College was enabled to recognise him in other ways,

however. He was appointed to the mastership of
Spalding School in Lincolnshire. At the end of about a
year, he quitted this post for one which offered attractions
of a different kind. Dr Stillingfleet—then Dean of St
Paul's, and formerly a Fellow of St John's, Cambridge—
wanted a tutor for his second son : and his choice fell on
Bentley.

A youth of twenty-one, with Bentley's tastes and
powers, could scarcely have been placed in a more ad-
vantageous position. Stillingfleet was already foremost
among those scholarly divines who were regarded as the ·
champions of Christianity against deists or materialists,
and more particularly as defenders of the English Church
against designs which had been believed to menace it since
the Restoration. The researches embodied in Stillingfleet's
Origines Sacrae and other works had for their general aim
to place the Anglican religion on the historical basis of
primitive times. In the course of his extensive and
varied studies, he had gradually formed that noble
library—one of the finest private collections then existing
in England—which after his death was purchased for
Dublin by Archbishop Marsh. Free access to such a
library was a priceless boon for Bentley. At the Dean's
house he would also meet the best literary society in
London ; and his 'patron'—to use the phrase of that
day—received him on a footing which enabled him to
profit fully by such opportunities. Stillingfleet could
sympathise with the studies of his son's young tutor. In
his own early days, after taking his degree at the same
College, Stillingfleet had accepted a domestic tutorship,
and 'besides his attendance on his proper province, the
instruction of the young gentleman,' had found time to
set about writing his *Irenicum*,—the endeavour of a

sanguine youth to make peace between Presbyterians
and Prelacy. A contemporary biographer (Dr Timothy
Goodwin) has thus described Dr Stillingfleet.   'He was
tall, graceful, and well-proportioned; his countenance
comely, fresh, and awful; in his conversation, cheerful
and discreet, obliging, and very instructive.' To the day
of his death in 1699 Stillingfleet was Bentley's best
friend,—the architect, indeed, of his early fortunes.

The next six years, from the twenty-first to the twenty-
seventh of his age (1683—1689), were passed by Bentley
in Dr Stillingfleet's family. It was during this period,
when he enjoyed much leisure and the use of a first-rate
library, that Bentley laid the solid foundations of his
learning. He enlarged his study of the Greek and Latin
classics, writing notes in the margin of his books as he
went along. In those days, it will be remembered, such
studies were not facilitated by copious dictionaries of
classical biography, geography, and antiquities, or by
those well-ordered and comprehensive lexicons which
exhibit at a glance the results attained by the labours of
successive generations. Bentley now began to make for
himself lists of the authors whom he found cited by the
ancient grammarians; and it may be observed that a series
of detractors, from Boyle's allies to Richard Dawes,
constantly twit Bentley with owing all his learning to
'indexes.' Thus, in a copy of verses preserved by Granger,
Bentley figures as

> Zoilus, tir'd with turning o'er
> Dull indexes, a precious store.

At this time he also studied the New Testament critically.
His labours on the Old Testament may be described in
his own words. 'I wrote, before I was twenty-four years

of age, a sort of *Hexapla;* a thick volume in quarto, in
the first column of which I inserted every word of the
Hebrew Bible alphabetically; and, in five other columns,
all the various interpretations of those words in the
Chaldee, Syriac, Vulgate, Latin, Septuagint, and Aquila,
Symmachus, and Theodotion, that occur in the whole
Bible.'

Bentley did not take Orders till 1690, when he was
twenty-eight, but he had probably always intended to do
so. His delay may have been partly due to the troubles
of James II.'s reign. Immediately after the Revolution
Dean Stillingfleet was raised to the see of Worcester.
His eldest son had gone to Cambridge; but Bentley's
pupil, James, was sent to Wadham College, Oxford.
Bentley accompanied him thither; and, having taken an
ad eundem degree of M.A., was placed on the books of
Wadham College. He continued to reside at Oxford till
the latter part of 1690; and we find him engaged on
behalf of the University in negotiations for the purchase
of the library which had belonged to Dr Isaac Voss,
Canon of Windsor. This valuable collection—including
the books of Gerard John Voss, Isaac's father—ultimately
went to Leyden; not, apparently, through any fault of
Bentley's, though that was alleged during his controversy
with Boyle.

While living at Oxford, Bentley enjoyed access to
the Bodleian Library; and, as if his ardour had been
stimulated by a survey of its treasures, it is at this
time that his literary projects first come into view. 'I
had decided' (he informs Dr Mill) 'to edit the fragments
of all the Greek poets, with emendations and notes, as a
single great work.' Perhaps even Bentley can scarcely
then have realised the whole magnitude of such a task,

and would have gauged it more accurately two years
later, when he had edited the fragments of Callimachus.
Nor was this the only vast scheme that floated before his
mind. In a letter to Dr Edward Bernard (then Savilian
Professor of Astronomy at Oxford) he discloses a project
of editing three Greek lexicons—those of Hesychius and
Suidas, with the *Etymologicum Magnum*—in three parallel
columns for each page. These would make three folio
volumes; a fourth volume would contain other lexicons
(as those of Julius Pollux, Erotian, and Phrynichus) which
did not lend themselves to the arrangement in column.
His thoughts were also busy with Philostratus (the Greek
biographer of the Sophists),—with Lucretius,—and with
the astronomical poet Manilius. Bentley excelled all
previous scholars in accurate knowledge of the classical
metres. His sojourn at Oxford is the earliest moment
at which we find a definite notice of his metrical studies.
The Baroccian collection in the Bodleian Library contains some manuscripts of the Greek 'Handbook of
Metres' which has come down under the name of the
grammarian Hephaestion. Bentley now collated these,
using a copy of the edition of Turnebus, in which he
made some marginal notes; the book is in the Library
of Trinity College, Cambridge.

When Bentley was thirty-six, he could still say, 'I
have never published anything yet, but at the desire of
others.' Before he left Oxford, towards the end of 1690,
a friend had already engaged him to appear in print.
The Baroccian collection of manuscripts contained the
only known copy of a chronicle written in Greek by
a certain John of Antioch. He is sometimes called John
Malelas, or simply Malelas. This is the Greek form of
a Syriac surname similar in import to the Greek *rhetor*,—

'orator,' 'eloquent writer.' It was given to other literary
men also, and merely served to distinguish this John of
Antioch from other well-known men of the same name
and place. His date is uncertain, but may probably be
placed between the seventh and tenth centuries. His
chronicle is a work of the kind which was often undertaken by Christian compilers. Beginning from the creation, he sought to give a chronological sketch of universal
history down to his own time. The work, as extant, is
incomplete. It begins with a statement characteristic of
its general contents ;—'After the death of Hephaestus
(Vulcan), his son Helius (the Sun) reigned over the
Egyptians for the space of 4407 days ;'—and it breaks off
at the year 560 A.D., five years before the death of
Justinian. Historically it is worthless, except in so far
as it preserves a few notices by writers contemporary
with the later emperors ; and it has no merit of form.
Scaliger once described a similar chronicle as a dust-bin.
Yet the mass of rubbish accumulated by John of Antioch
includes a few fragments of better things. Not only the
classical prose-writers but the classical poets were among
his authorities, for he made no attempt to discriminate
facts from myths. In several places he preserves the
names of lost works. Here and there, too, a bit of
classical prose or verse has stuck in the dismal swamp of
his text. Eager to reconstruct ancient chronology, the
students of the seventeenth century had not overlooked
this unattractive author. In the reign of Charles I.
two Oxford scholars had successively studied him. John
Gregory (who died in 1646) had proved the authorship of
the chronicle—mutilated though it was at both ends—by
showing that a passage of it is elsewhere quoted as from
the chronicle of Malelas. Edmund Chilmead,—a man

remarkable for his attainments in scholarship, mathematics, and music,—translated it into Latin, adding
notes. As a royalist, Chilmead was ejected from Christ
Church by the Parliamentary Visitation of 1648. He
died in 1653, just as his work was ready to be printed.
After the lapse of thirty-eight years, the Curators of the
Sheldonian Press resolved in 1690 to edit it. The manuscript chronicle had already gained some repute through the
citations of it by such scholars as Selden, Usher, Pearson,
Stanley, Lloyd. It was arranged that an introduction
should be written by Humphrey Hody, who had been
James Stillingfleet's College tutor at Wadham, and had,
like Bentley, been appointed Chaplain to the Bishop of
Worcester. He was an excellent scholar, and performed
his task in a highly creditable manner. A general
supervision of the edition had been entrusted to Dr John
Mill, Principal of St Edmund Hall, whose learning has
an abiding monument in his subsequent edition of the New
Testament. One day Mill and Bentley were walking
together at Oxford, when the conversation turned on the
chronicle of Malelas. Bentley said that he would like to
see the book before it was published. Mill consented, on
condition that Bentley would communicate any suggestions
that might occur to him. The proof-sheets were then
sent to Bentley; who shortly afterwards left Oxford, to
take up his residence as chaplain with the Bishop of
Worcester.

Dr Mill presently claimed Bentley's promise; and,
thus urged, Bentley at length sent his remarks on
Malelas, in the form of a Latin Letter addressed to Dr
Mill. He elsewhere says that he had been further pressed
to write it by the learned Bishop Lloyd. In June, 1691,
the chronicle appeared, with Bentley's Letter to Mill

as an appendix. This edition ('Oxonii, e Theatro
Sheldoniano') is a moderately thick octavo volume; first
stands a note by Hody, on the spelling of the chronicler's
surname; then his Prolegomena, filling 64 pages; the
Greek text follows, with Chilmead's Latin version in
parallel columns, and foot-notes; and the last 98 pages
are occupied by Bentley's Letter to Mill.

Briefly observing that he leaves to Hody the question
of the chronicler's identity and age, Bentley comes at
once to the text. Malelas had treated Greek mythology
as history, interweaving it with other threads of ancient
record. Thus, after enumerating some fabulous kings of
Attica, he proceeds: 'Shortly afterwards, Gideon was
leader of Israel. Contemporary with him was the famous
lyric poet Orpheus, of Thrace.' Malelas then quotes some
statements as to the mystic theology taught by Orpheus.
One of these is a sentence which, as he gives it, seems to
be composed of common words, but is wholly unintelligible.
Bentley takes up this sentence. He shows that the deeply
corrupted words conceal the names of three mystic
divinities in the later Orphic system, symbolical, respectively, of *Counsel, Light,* and *Life.* He proves this
emendation, as certain as it is wonderful, by quoting a
passage from Damascius,—the last great Neoplatonist, who
lived in the early part of the sixth century, and wrote a
treatise called 'Questions and Answers on First Principles,'
in which he sketches the theology of 'the current Orphic
rhapsodies.' This treatise was not even partially printed
till 1828; and Bentley quotes it from a manuscript in
the library of Corpus Christi College, Oxford. He next
deals with a group of fictitious 'oracles' which Malelas
had reduced from hexameter verse into prose of the
common dialect, and shows that several of them closely

resemble some which he had found in a manuscript at
Oxford, entitled 'Oracles and Theologies of Greek
Philosophers.'

Then he turns to those passages in which the chronicle
cites the Attic dramatists. He demonstrates the spuriousness of a fragment ascribed to Sophocles. He confirms or corrects the titles of several lost plays which
Malelas ascribes to Euripides, and incidentally amends
numerous passages which he has occasion to quote. Dis-
cursive exuberance of learning characterises the whole
Letter. A single example will serve to illustrate it.
Malelas says: 'Euripides brought out a play about
Pasiphaë.' Bentley remarks on this: 'I do not speak at
random; and I am certain that *no* ancient writer mentions
a Pasiphaë of Euripides.' The comic poet Alcaeus, indeed,
composed a piece of that name, which is said to have been
exhibited in the same year as the recast *Plutus* of
Aristophanes. It is true, however, Bentley adds, that
the *story* of Pasiphaë had been handled by Euripides,
in a lost play called *The Cretans*. This he proves from
a scholiast on the *Frogs* of Aristophanes. But the
scholiast himself needs correction: who says that Euripides introduced Aeropè in *The Cretans*. Here he
is confounding *The Cretans* with another lost play of
Euripides, called the *Women of Crete*: the former dealt
with the story of Icarus and Pasiphaë, the latter with
that of Aeropè, Atreus and Thyestes. Porphyry, in his
book on Abstinence, quotes nine verses from a play of
Euripides, in which the chorus are addressing Minos.
Grotius, in his Excerpts from Greek Comedies and Trage-
dies, had attempted to amend these corrupted verses, and
had supposed them to come from the *Women of Crete*.
Bentley (incidentally correcting a grammarian) demon-

strates that they can have belonged only to *The Cretans.*
He then turns to the Greek verses themselves. Grotius
had given a Latin version of them, in the same metre.
This metre was the anapæstic—one which had been
frequently used by the scholars of the sixteenth and
seventeenth centuries, both in translations and in original
poems. Bentley points out that one of its most essential
laws had been ignored, not only by Grotius, but by the
modern Latinists generally, including Joseph Scaliger.
The ancients regarded the verses of this metre as forming
a continuous chain; hence the last syllable of a verse
was not indifferently long or short, but necessarily one or
the other, as if it occurred in the middle of a verse.
Thus Grotius had written :—

> Quas prisca domos dedit indigena
> Quercus Chalyba secta bipenni.

Here the short *a* at the end of *indigena* should be a
long syllable, in order to make an anapæst (◡◡−). This
is known as Bentley's discovery of the *synaphea* ('con-
nection') in anapæstic verse. He further illustrates the
metre from fragments of the Latin poet Attius,—which
he amends; one fragment, indeed, he recognises in the
prose of Cicero's *Tusculans.* Returning to the fragment
of *The Cretans* in Porphyry, which Grotius had handled
amiss, Bentley corrects it,—with certainty in some points,
with rashness in others, but everywhere brilliantly. Nor
has he done with the verses yet. They mention the
cypress as 'native' to Crete. This leads Bentley to
discuss and amend passages in Pliny's Natural History,
in the History of Plants by Theophrastus, and in the
geographical work of Solinus.

Elsewhere Malelas refers to the lost *Meleager* of
Euripides. Having quoted another mention of it from

Hesychius, Bentley takes occasion to show at length the
principal causes of error in that lexicon. This is one of
the most striking parts of the Letter. Then, in numerous
places, he restores proper names which Malelas had defaced. The chronicler says that the earliest dramatists
were Themis, Minos, and Auleas. Bentley shows that
he means Thespis, Ion of Chios, and Aeschylus. Thespis
leads him to quote Clement of Alexandria, and to explain
some mysterious words by showing that they are
specimens of a pastime which consisted in framing a
sentence with the twenty-four letters of the alphabet,
each used once only. Speaking of Ion, he gives an
exhaustive discussion of that poet's date and writings,
verse and prose. The Letter ends with some remarks on
the form of the name *Malelas.* Hody had found fault
with Bentley for adding the final *s*, which no previous
scholar used. Bentley replies that *a* at the end of a
foreign name ordinarily became *as* in Greek,—as *Agrippas.*
And Malelas being the Greek form of a Greek writer's
name, we should keep it in Latin and English, just as
Cicero says *Lysias,* not *Lysia.* The Latin exceptions are
the domesticated names,—those of slaves, or of Greeks
naturalised by residence : as *Sosia, Phania.* But it was
objected that *Malela* was a 'barbarian' name, and therefore indeclinable. Bentley answers that the Hun Attila
appears in Greek writers as *Attilas,*—adding half-a-dozen
Huns, Goths, and Vandals. The prejudice in favour of
Malela arose from a simple cause. The chronicler is
mentioned only thrice by Greek writers : two of these
three passages happen to have the name in the genitive
case, which is *Malela ;* the third, however, has the nomi-
native, which is *Malelas.* Mr Hody was not convinced
about the *s.* The note—in four large pages of small

print—which precedes his Prolegomena was written after he had read Bentley's argument; and ends with a prayer. Mr Hody's aspiration is that *he* may always write in a becoming spirit; and, finally, that he may be a despiser of trifles (*nugarum denique contemptor*).

Taken as a whole, Bentley's Letter to Mill is an extraordinary performance for a scholar of twenty-eight in the year 1690. It ranges from one topic to another over almost the whole field of ancient literature. Upwards of sixty Greek and Latin writers, from the earliest to the latest, are incidentally explained or corrected. There are many curious tokens of the industry with which Bentley had used his months at Oxford. Thus, referring to a manuscript of uncertain origin in the Bodleian Library, 'I have made out,' he says, 'from some iambics at the beginning,—almost effaced by age—that it contains the work of the grammarian Theognotus, whom the author of the *Etymologicum Magnum* quotes several times;' and he gives his proof.

It is interesting to see how strongly this first production bears the stamp of that peculiar style which afterwards marked Bentley's criticism. It is less the style of a writer than of a speaker who is arguing in a strain of rough vivacity with another person. The tone is often as if the ancient author was reading his composition aloud to Bentley, but making stupid mistakes through drowsiness or inattention. Bentley pulls him up short; remonstrates with him in a vein of good-humoured sarcasm; points out to him that he can scarcely mean *this*, but—as his own words elsewhere prove—must, no doubt, have meant *that;* and recommends him to think more of logic. Sometimes it is the modern reader whom Bentley addresses, as if begging him to be calm in

the face of some tremendous blunder just committed by
the ancient author, who is intended to overhear the
'aside :'—'Do not mind him ; he does not really mean it.
He is like this sometimes, and makes us anxious ; but he
has plenty of good sense, if one can only get at it. Let
us see what we can do for him.' This colloquial manner,
with its alternating appeals to author and reader, in
one instance exposed Bentley to an unmerited rebuke
from Dr Monk. Once, after triumphantly showing that
John of Antioch supposed the Boeotian Aulis to be in
Scythia, Bentley exclaims, *'Good indeed, Johnny !'* (Euge
vero, ὦ 'Ιωαννίδιον). Dr Monk thought that this was said
to Dr John Mill, and reproved it as 'an indecorum which
neither the familiarity of friendship, nor the license of a
dead language, can justify towards the dignified Head
of a House.' Mr Maehly, in a memoir of Bentley,
rejoins : 'That may be the view of English high life ; a
German savant would never have been offended by the
expressions in question.' (Das mag Anschauung des
englischen *high life* sein : einem deutschen Gelehrten
würden die fraglichen Ausdrücke nie aufgefallen sein.)
But our Aristarchus was not addressing the Principal of
St Edmund Hall; he was sportively upbraiding the
ancient chronicler. Indeed, Monk's slip—a thing most
rare in his work—was pointed out in a review of his
first edition, and is absent from the second.

Two of the first scholars of that day—John George
Graevius and Ezechiel Spanheim—separately saluted the
young author of the Letter to Mill as 'a new and already
bright star' of English letters. But the Letter to Mill
received by far its most memorable tribute, years after
Bentley's death, from David Ruhnken, in his preface to
the Hesychius of Alberti. 'Those great men,' he says—

J. B.   C

meaning such scholars as Scaliger, Casaubon, Saumaise
—'did not dare to say openly what they thought (about
Hesychius),—whether deterred by the established repute
of the grammarian, or by the clamours of the half-learned,
who are always noisy against their betters, and who were
uneasy at the notion of the great Hesychius losing his
pre-eminence.   In order that the truth should be published and proved, we needed the learned daring of
Richard Bentley,—daring which here, if anywhere,
served literature better than the sluggish and credulous
superstition of those who wish to be called and deemed
critics.   Bentley shook off the servile yoke, and put forth
that famous *Letter to Mill*,—a wonderful monument of
genius and learning, such as could have come only from
the first critic of his time.'

CHAPTER II.

ROBERT BOYLE, born in the year after Bacon's death (1627), stands next to him among the Englishmen of the seventeenth century who advanced inductive science. His experiments—'physico-mechanical,' as he describes them—led to the discovery of the law for the elasticity of the air; improvements in the air-pump and the thermometer were due to him; and his investigations were serviceable to Hydrostatics, Chemistry, and Medicine. In his theological writings it was his chief aim to show 'the reconcilableness of reason and religion,' and thus to combat the most powerful prejudice which opposed the early progress of the New Philosophy. Boyle's mind, like Newton's, became more profoundly reverent the further he penetrated into the secrets of nature; his innermost feeling appears to be well represented by the title which he chose for one of his essays—'On the high veneration man's intellect owes to God, peculiarly for his wisdom and power.' Thus his 'Disquisition on Final Causes' was designed to prove, as against inferences which had been drawn from the cosmical system of Descartes, that the structure of the universe reveals the work of a divine

c 2

intelligence. Dying on December 30, 1691, he left a
bequest which was in harmony with the main purpose of
his life, and which might be regarded as his personal and
permanent protest against the idea that a servant of
science is an enemy of religion.

He assigned fifty pounds a year as a stipend 'for some
divine, or preaching minister,' who should 'preach eight
Sermons in the year for proving the Christian religion
against notorious infidels, viz. Atheists, Deists, Pagans,
Jews, and Mahometans; *not descending to any controversies
that are among Christians themselves:* The lectures to be
on the first Monday of the respective months of January,
February, March, April, May, September, October,
November; in such church as the trustees shall from
time to time appoint.' The four trustees named in the
will—Bishop Tenison, Sir Henry Ashurst, Sir John
Rotheram, and John Evelyn (the author of the *Sylva*
and the *Diary*)—soon appointed the Lecturer who was
to deliver the first course. 'We made choice of one
Mr Bentley,' says Evelyn,—'chaplain to the Bishop of
Worcester.' Bishop Stillingfleet, himself so eminent an
apologist, would naturally be consulted in such an
election.

Bentley took for his subject the first of the topics
indicated by the founder :—'A confutation of Atheism.'
At this time the *Leviathan* of Thomas Hobbes had been
forty years before the world: and Bentley's lectures
stand in a peculiar relation to it. Hobbes resolved all ideas
into sensations; he denied that there was 'any common rule
of good and evil, to be taken from the nature of the objects
themselves.' He did *not*, however, deny the existence of
a God. 'Curiosity about causes,' says Hobbes, 'led men
to search out, one after the other, till they came to the

necessary conclusion, that there is some eternal cause
which men called God. But they have no more idea of
his nature than a blind man has of fire, though he knows
that there is something which warms him.' So elsewhere
he distinguishes between the necessary 'acknowledgment
of one infinite, omnipotent and eternal God,' and the
attempt—which he pronounces delusive—to define the
nature of that Being 'by spirit incorporeal.'

Bentley held with those who regarded Hobbes, not
merely as a materialist who destroyed the basis of
morality, but as an atheist in the disguise of a deist.
Writing to Bernard, Bentley says roundly of Hobbes,
'his corporeal God is a meer sham to get his book
printed.' Hobbes had said—not in the *Leviathan*, but
in 'An Answer to Bishop Bramhall,' who had pressed
him on this point—'I maintain God's existence, and that
he is a most pure and most simple *corporeal spirit:*'
adding, 'by corporeal I mean a substance that has magnitude.' Elsewhere he adds '*invisible*' before 'corporeal.' But at this time the suspicion of a tendency
was sometimes enough to provoke the charge of atheism:
thus Cudworth, in his *Intellectual System*—published
fourteen years before Bentley's lectures, and, like them,
directed mainly against Hobbes—casts the imputation,
without a shadow of reason, on Gassendi, Descartes,
and Bacon. Bentley declared that atheism was rife
in 'taverns and coffee-houses, nay Westminster-hall and
the very churches.' The school of Hobbes, he was
firmly persuaded, was answerable for this. 'There may
be some Spinosists, or immaterial Fatalists, beyond seas,'
says Bentley; 'but not one English infidel in a hundred
is any other than a Hobbist; which I know to be rank
atheism in the private study and select conversation of

those men, whatever it may appear abroad.' Bentley's
Lectures are, throughout, essentially an argument against
Hobbes. The set of the lecturer's thoughts may be seen
from an illustration used in his second discourse, where
he is arguing against a fortuitous origin of the universe.
'If a man should affirm that an ape, casually meeting
with pen, ink, and paper, and falling to scribble, did
happen to write exactly the *Leviathan* of Thomas Hobbes,
would an atheist believe such a story?'

It was from the pulpit of St Martin's Church, in
London, that Bentley delivered his Boyle Lectures. The
first was given on March 7, 1692. Bentley announces
that his refutation of atheists will not be drawn from
those sacred books which, in their eyes, possess no
special authority; 'but, however, there are other books
extant, which they must needs allow of as proper
evidence; even the mighty volumes of visible nature, and
the everlasting tables of right reason; wherein, if they do
not wilfully shut their eyes, they may read their own
folly written by the finger of God, in a much plainer and
more terrible sentence than Belshazzar's was by the hand
upon the wall.'

In choosing this ground Bentley was following a recent example. Richard Cumberland, afterwards Bishop of
Peterborough, had published in 1672 his 'Philosophical
Disquisition on the Laws of Nature'—arguing, against
the school of Hobbes, that certain immutable principles
of moral choice are inherent in the nature of things and
in the mind of man. He purposely refrains, however,
from appealing to Scripture: the testimony which
Cumberland invokes is that of recent science, mathematical or physiological,—of Descartes and Huygens, of
Willis or Harvey. It is characteristic of Bentley that

he chose to draw his weapons from the same armoury. He was already a disciple of strictly theological learning. But in this field, as in others, he declined to use authority as a refuge from logical encounter.

Bentley's first Lecture argues that to adopt atheism is 'to choose death and evil before life and good;' that such folly is needless, since religion imposes nothing repugnant to man's faculties or incredible to his reason; that it is also hurtful, both to the individual, whom it robs of the best hope, and to communities, since religion is the basis of society. The second Lecture proceeds to deduce the existence of the Deity from the faculties of the human soul. Hobbes had said: 'There is no conception in a man's mind which hath not at first, totally or by parts, been begotten upon the organs of sense: the rest are derived from that original.' Bentley, on the contrary, undertakes to prove that 'the powers of cogitation, and volition, and sensation, are neither inherent in matter as such, nor producible in matter;' but proceed from 'some cogitative substance, some incorporeal inhabitant within us, which we call spirit and soul.' As the result of the inquiry, he concludes that there is 'an immaterial and intelligent Being, that created our souls; which Being was either eternal itself, or created immediately or ultimately by some other Eternal, that has all those perfections. There is, therefore, originally an eternal, immaterial, intelligent Creator; all which together are the attributes of God alone.' Evelyn, who was present at this Lecture, writes of it in his *Diary* (April 4, 1692)—'*one of the most learned and convincing discourses I had ever heard.*' From this point we may date the friendship which till his death in 1706 he steadily entertained for Bentley. The third, fourth and fifth Lectures

urge the same inference from the origin and structure of
human bodies. Bentley seeks to prove that 'the human
race was neither from everlasting without beginning; nor
owes its beginning to the influence of heavenly bodies;
nor to what they call nature, that is, the necessary and
mechanical motions of dead senseless matter.' His style
of argument on the evidence of design in the human
structure may be seen from this passage on the organism
of the heart:—

'If we consider the heart, which is supposed to be
the first principle of motion and life, and divide it by our
imagination into its constituent parts, its arteries, and
veins, and nerves, and tendons, and membranes, and innu-
merable little fibres that these secondary parts do consist
of, we shall find nothing here singular, but what is in any
other muscle of the body. 'Tis only the site and posture
of these several parts, and the configuration of the whole,
that give it the form and functions of a heart. Now,
why should the first single fibres in the formation of the
heart be peculiarly drawn in spiral lines, when the fibres
of all other muscles are made by a transverse rectilinear
motion? What could determine the fluid matter into that
odd and singular figure, when as yet no other member is
supposed to be formed, that might direct the course of
that fluid matter? Let mechanism here make an experiment of its power, and produce a spiral and turbinated
motion of the whole moved body without an external
director.'

The last three Lectures (vi., vii., viii.) deal with the
proofs from 'the origin and frame of the world.' These
are by far the most striking of the series. Newton's
Principia had now been published for five years. But,
beyond the inner circle of scientific students, the

Cartesian system was still generally received. Descartes taught that each planet was carried round the sun in a separate vortex; and that the satellites are likewise carried round by smaller vortices, contained within those of the several planets. Centrifugal motion would constantly impel the planets to fly off in a straight line from the sun; but they are kept in their orbits by the pressure of an outer sphere, consisting of denser particles which are beyond the action of the vortices.

Newton had demolished this theory. He had shown that the planets are held in their orbits by the force of *gravity*, which is always drawing them towards the sun, combined with a *transverse impulse*, which is always projecting them at tangents to their orbits. Bentley takes up Newton's great discovery, and applies it to prove the existence of an Intelligent Providence. Let us grant, he says, that the force of gravity is inherent to matter. What can have been the origin of that other force,—the transverse impulse? This impulse is not uniform, but has been adjusted to the place of each body in the system. Each planet has its particular velocity, proportioned to its distance from the sun and to the quantity of the solar matter. It can be due to one cause alone—an intelligent and omnipotent Creator.

This view has the express sanction of Newton. His letters to Bentley—subsequent in date to the Lectures—repeatedly confirm it. 'I do not know any power in nature,' Newton writes, 'which would cause this transverse motion without the divine arm.'...'To make this system, with all its motions, required a cause which understood and compared together the quantities of matter in the several bodies of the sun and planets, and the gravitating powers resulting from thence; the

several distances of the primary planets from the sun,
and of the secondary ones from Saturn, Jupiter, and the
Earth; and the velocities with which these planets could
revolve about those quantities of matter in the central
bodies; and to compare and adjust all these things together, in so great a variety of bodies, argues that cause
to be, not blind and fortuitous, but very well skilled in
mechanics and geometry.'

The application of Newton's discoveries which Bentley
makes in the Boyle Lectures was peculiarly welcome to
Newton himself. 'When I wrote my treatise about our
system,' he says to Bentley, 'I had an eye upon such
principles as might work with considering men for the
belief of a Deity; and nothing can rejoice me more than
to find it useful for that purpose. But if I have done the
public any service this way, it is due to nothing but
industry and patient thought.'

The correspondence between Bentley and Newton,
to which the Boyle Lectures gave rise, would alone
make them memorable. It has commonly been supposed
that Bentley first studied the *Principia* with a view to
these Lectures. This, as I can prove, is an error.
The Library of Trinity College, Cambridge, contains
the autographs of Newton's four letters to Bentley,
and of his directions for reading the *Principia;* also a
letter to Wotton from John Craig, a Scottish mathematician, giving advice on the same subject, for
Bentley's benefit. Now, Craig's letter is dated June
24, 1691; Bentley, then, must have turned his mind
to the *Principia* six months before the Boyle Lectures
were even founded. We know, further, that in 1689 he
was working on Lucretius. I should conjecture, then,
that his first object in studying Newton's cosmical system

had been to compare it with that of Epicurus, as interpreted by Lucretius; to whom, indeed, he refers more than once in the Boyle Lectures. Craig gives an alarming list of books which must be read before the *Principia* can be understood, and represents the study as most arduous. Newton's own directions to Bentley are simple and encouraging: 'at ye first perusal of my Book,' he concludes, 'it's enough if you understand y^u Propositions wth some of y^u Demonstrations wch are easier than the rest. For when you understand ye easier, they will afterwards give you light into ye harder.' At the bottom of the paper Bentley has written, in his largest and boldest character, '*Directions from Mr Newton by his own Hand.*' There is no date. Clearly, however, it was Craig's formidable letter which determined Bentley on writing to Newton. The rapidity with which Bentley—among all his other pursuits—comprehended the *Principia* proves both industry and power. Some years later, his Lectures were searched for flaws by John Keill, afterwards Savilian Professor of Astronomy at Oxford, and the principal agent in introducing Newton's system there. The Phalaris controversy was going on, and Keill wished to damage Bentley. But he could find only one real blot. Bentley had missed Newton's discovery—mentioned, but not prominent, in the *Principia*—that the moon revolves about her own axis. Keill's only other point was a verbal cavil, refuted by the context. Better testimony to Bentley's accuracy could scarcely have been borne.

The last Lecture was given on December 5, 1692. The first six had already been printed. But before publishing the last two—which dealt in more detail with Newton's principles—Bentley wished to consult Newton

himself. He therefore wrote to him, at Trinity College,
Cambridge. It was in the autumn of that year that
Newton had finished his Letters on Fluxions. He was
somewhat out of health, suffering from sleeplessness and
loss of appetite; perhaps (as his letters to Locke suggest)
vexed by the repeated failure of his friends to obtain for
him such a provision as he desired. But he at once
answered Bentley's letter with that concise and lucid
thoroughness which makes his style a model in its kind.
His first letter is dated Dec. 10, 1692, and addressed to
Bentley 'at the Bishop of Worcester's House, in Park-
Street in Westminster.' On the back of it Bentley has
written:—'Mr Newton's Answer to some Queries sent
by me, after I had preach't my 2 last Sermons; All his
answers are agreeable to what I had deliver'd before in
the pulpit. But of some incidental things I do ἐπέχειν
[suspend judgment]. R.B.' Three other letters are extant
which Newton wrote at this time to Bentley,—the last,
on Feb. 25, 1693. He probably wrote others also;
there are several from Bentley to him in the Portsmouth
collection.

In the course of these four letters, Newton approves
nearly all the arguments for the existence of God which
Bentley had deduced from the *Principia.* On one
important point, however, he corrects him. Bentley
had conceded to the atheists that gravity may be
essential and inherent to matter. 'Pray,' says Newton,
'do not ascribe that notion to me; for the cause of gravity
is what I do not pretend to know, and therefore would
take more time to consider of it.' In the last letter,
about five weeks later, Newton returns to this topic, and
speaks more decidedly. The notion of gravity being
inherent to matter 'is to me,' he says, 'so great an

absurdity, that I believe no man, who has in philosophical matters any competent faculty of thinking, can ever fall into it. Gravity must be caused by an agent acting constantly according to certain laws; but whether this agent be material or immaterial, I have left to the consideration of my readers.'

One of the most interesting points in these letters is to see how a mind like Bentley's, so wonderfully acute in certain directions, and logical in criticism even to excess, is corrected by a mathematical mind. Thus Bentley, in writing to Newton, had argued that every particle of matter in an infinite space has an infinite quantity of matter on all sides, and consequently an infinite attraction every way; it must therefore rest in equilibrium, all infinites being equal. Now, says Newton, by similar reasoning we might prove that an inch is equal to a foot. For, if an inch may be divided into an infinite number of parts, the sum of those parts will be an inch; and if a foot may be divided into an infinite number of parts, the sum of those parts must be a foot; and therefore, since all infinites are equal, those sums must be equal; that is, an inch must be equal to a foot. The logic is strict; what, then, is the error in the premises? The position, Newton answers, that all infinites are equal. Infinites may be considered in two ways. Viewed absolutely, they are neither equal nor unequal. But when considered under certain definite restrictions, as mathematics may consider them, they can be compared. 'A mathematician would tell you that, though there be an infinite number of infinite little parts in an inch, yet there is twelve times that number of such parts in a foot.' And so Bentley's infinite attracting forces must be so conceived as if the

addition of the slightest finite attracting force to either
would destroy the equilibrium.

Johnson has observed that these letters show 'how
even the mind of Newton gains ground gradually upon
darkness:' a fine remark, but one which will convey an
incorrect impression if it is supposed to mean that
Bentley's questions had led Newton to modify or extend
any doctrine set forth in the *Principia.* Bentley's present
object in using the *Principia* was to refute atheism.
Newton had not previously considered all the possible
applications of his own discoveries to the purposes of
theological controversy.   This is the limit to the novelty
of suggestion which he found in Bentley's letters.   Besides
the few cases in which Newton points out a fallacy, there
are others in which he puts a keener edge on some argument propounded by his correspondent.   For instance,
Bentley had submitted some reasons against 'the hypothesis of deriving the frame of the world by mechanical
principles from matter evenly spread through the heavens.'
This was one of the theories which sought to eliminate the
necessity of an intelligent cause.   It was, of course, radi-
cally incompatible with Newton's system.   'I had considered it very little,' Newton writes, 'before your letters
put me upon it.'   But then he goes on to point out how
it may be urned against its authors.   It involves the
assumption that gravity is inherent to matter.   But, if this
is so, then matter could never have been evenly spread
through the heavens, without the intervention of a super-
natural power.

Newton's letters, while they heighten our admiration
for the master, also illustrate the great ability of the
disciple,—his strong grasp of a subject which lay beyond
the sphere of his familiar studies, and his vigorous

originality in the use of new acquisitions. Bentley's
Boyle Lectures have a lasting worth which is independent of their scientific value as an argument. In
regard to the latter, it may be observed that they bear
the mark of their age in their limited conception of a
natural law as distinguished from a personal agency.
Thus gravitation is allowed as a natural 'law' because its
action is constant and uniform. But wherever there is a
more and a less, wherever the operation is apparently
variable, this is explained by the intervening will of an
intelligent person; it is not conceived that the disturbing
or modifying force may be another, though unknown,
'law,' in the sense in which that name is given to a
manifestly regular sequence of cause and effect. On
their literary side, the best parts of the Lectures exhibit
Bentley as a born controversialist, and the worst as a
born litigant. The latter character appears in an
occasional tendency to hair-splitting and quibbling; the
former, in his sustained power of terse and animated
reasoning, in rapid thrust and alert defence, in ready
command of various resources, in the avoidance of
declamation while he is proving his point, and in the
judicious use of eloquence to clinch it. Here, as elsewhere, he has the knack of illustrating an abstruse subject
by an image from common things. He is touching (in
the second Lecture) on the doctrine of Epicurus that
our freedom of will is due to the declension of atoms
from the perpendicular as they fall through infinite
space. ' 'Tis as if one should say that a bowl equally
poised, and thrown upon a plain and smooth bowling-
green, will run necessarily and fatally in a direct motion;
but if it be made with a bias, that may decline it a
little from a straight line, it may acquire by that motion

a liberty of will, and so run spontaneously to the jack.'
It may be noticed that a passage in the eighth Lecture is
one of the quaintest testimonies in literature to the
comparatively recent origin of a taste for the grander
forms of natural scenery. Bentley supposes his adversaries to object that 'the rugged and irregular surface'
of the earth refutes its claim to be 'a work of divine
artifice.' 'We ought not to believe,' he replies, 'that the
banks of the ocean are really deformed, because they
have not the form of a regular bulwark; nor that the
mountains are out of shape, because they are not exact
pyramids or cones.'

The Lectures made a deep and wide impression.
Soon after they had been published, a Latin version
appeared at Berlin. A Dutch version subsequently came
out at Utrecht. There was one instance, indeed, of
dissent from the general approval. A Yorkshire squire
wrote a pamphlet, intimating that his own experience
did not lead him to consider the faculties of the human
soul as a decisive argument for the existence of a Deity;
and, referring to Bentley's observations on this head, he
remarked, 'I judge he hath taken the wrong sow by the
ear.' In 1694 Bentley again delivered a course of Boyle
Lectures—'A Defence of Christianity'—but they were
never printed. Manuscript copies of them are mentioned
by Kippis, the editor of the *Biographia Britannica*
(1780): but Dean Vincent, who died in 1815, is reported
by Kidd as believing that they were lost.

CHAPTER III.

In 1692—the year of his first Boyle Lecturership—an
accident placed Bentley in correspondence with John
George Graevius, a German who held a professorship at
Utrecht, and stood in the front rank of classical—
especially Latin—scholarship. When Bentley was seeking materials for an edition of Manilius, he received
a box of papers from Sir Edward Sherburn, an old
cavalier who had partly translated the poet. The papers
in the box, bought at Antwerp, had belonged to the
Dutch scholar, Gaspar Gevärts. Among them was a Latin
tract by Albert Rubens ('Rubenius'), the author of
another treatise which Graevius had previously edited.
Bentley, with Sherburn's leave, sent the newly-found tract
to Graevius, who published it in 1694, with a dedication
to Bentley. This circumstance afterwards brought on
Bentley the absurd charge of having intercepted an
honour due to Sherburn.

Graevius was rejoiced to open a correspondence
with the author of the Letter to Mill, which he had
warmly admired. The professor's son had lately died,
leaving an unpublished edition of the Greek poet

Callimachus, which Graevius was now preparing to edit.
He applied to Bentley for any literary aid that he could
give. In reply, Bentley undertook to collect the fragments of Callimachus, scattered up and down throughout
Greek literature; remarking that he could promise to
double the number printed in a recent Paris edition, and
also to improve the text. In 1696 Bentley fulfilled this
promise by sending to Graevius a collection of about 420
fragments; also a new recension of the poet's epigrams,
with additions to their number from a fresh manuscript
source, and with some notes on the hymns. The edition
appeared at Utrecht in 1697, with Bentley's contributions.

In the preface Graevius shows his sense that the work
done by Bentley—'that new and brilliant light of
Britain'—was not merely excellent in quality, but of a
new order. Such indeed it was. Since then, successive
generations have laboured at collecting and sifting the
fragments of the Greek poets. But in 1697 the world
had no example of systematic work in this field. The
first pattern of thorough treatment and the first model of
critical method were furnished by Bentley's Callimachus.
Hitherto the collector of fragments had aimed at little
more than heaping together 'the limbs of the dis-
membered poet.' Bentley shows how these limbs, when
they have been gathered, may serve, within certain limits,
to reconstruct the body. Starting from a list of the
poet's works, extant or known by title, he aims at
arranging the fragments under those works to which
they severally belonged. But, while he concentrates his
critical resources in a methodical manner, he wisely
refrains from pushing conjecture too far. His Callimachus is hardly more distinguished by brilliancy than
by cautious judgment; praise which could not be given

to all his later works. Here, as in the Letter to Mill, we see his metrical studies bearing fruit: thus he points out a fact which had hitherto escaped even such scholars as Saumaise and Casaubon,—that the Greek diphthongs *ai* and *oi* cannot be shortened before consonants. Ernesti, in the preface to his Callimachus (1763), speaks of Bentley as 'having distanced competition:' and another estimate, of yet higher authority, is expressed more strongly still. 'Nothing more excellent in its kind has appeared,' said Valckenaer,—'nothing more highly finished;' 'a most thorough piece of work, by which writers who respect their readers might well be deterred' from an attempt at rivalry. It is no real abatement of Bentley's desert that a few gleanings were left for those who came after him. Here, as in some other cases, the distinctive merit of his work is not that it was final but that it was exemplary. In this particular department —the editing of fragments—he differed from his predecessors as the numismatist, who arranges a cabinet of coins, differs from the digger who is only aware that he has unearthed an old bit of gold or silver.

Meanwhile letters had been passing between Bentley and a correspondent very unlike Graevius. In 1693 Joshua Barnes, of Emmanuel College, Cambridge, was editing Euripides, and wrote to Bentley, asking his reasons for an opinion attributed to him,—that the 'Letters of Euripides' were spurious. Bentley gave these reasons in a long and courteous reply. Barnes, however, resented the loss of a cherished illusion. Not only did he omit to thank Bentley, but in the preface to his Euripides (1694) he alluded to his correspondent's opinion as 'a proof of effrontery or incapacity.' Barnes is a curious figure, half-comic half-pathetic, among the

minor persons of Bentley's story. Widely read, in-
cessantly laborious, but uncritical and vain, he poured
forth a continual stream of injudicious publications,
English or Greek, until, when he was fifty-one, they
numbered forty-three. The last work of his life was
an elaborate edition of Homer. He had invested the
fortune of Mrs Barnes in this costly enterprise,—obtaining her somewhat reluctant consent, it was said, by
representing the Iliad as the work of King Solomon.
Queen Anne declined the dedication, and nothing could
persuade poor Barnes that this was not Bentley's doing.
Bentley said of Barnes that he probably knew about
as much Greek, and understood it about as well, as
an Athenian blacksmith. The great critic appears to
have forgotten that Sophocles and Aristophanes were
appreciated by audiences which represented the pit
and the gallery much more largely than the boxes and
the stalls. An Athenian blacksmith could teach us a
good many things.

Bentley had now made his mark, and he had powerful friends. One piece of preferment after another came
to him. In 1692 Bishop Stillingfleet procured for him a
prebendal stall at Worcester, and three years later appointed him to hold the Rectory of Hartlebury, in that
county, until James Stillingfleet should be in full orders.
At the end of the year 1693 the office of Royal
Librarian became vacant. By an arrangement which
was not then thought singular, the new Librarian was
induced to resign in favour of Bentley, who was to pay
him £130 a year out of the salary of £200. The patent
appointing Bentley Keeper of the Royal Libraries bore
date April 12, 1694. The 'Licensing Act' (Stat. 13
and 14, Car. II.) finally expired in 1694, a few months

after Bentley took office. But he made the most of his time. The Act reserved three copies of every book printed in England,—one for the Royal Library, one for Oxford, and one for Cambridge. Latterly it had been evaded. Bentley applied to the Master of the Stationers' Company, and exacted '*near a thousand*' volumes. In this year he was elected a Fellow of the Royal Society. In 1695 he became a Chaplain in ordinary to the King. Hitherto he had resided with Bishop Stillingfleet: but early in 1696 he took possession of the rooms in St James's Palace which were assigned to the Royal Librarian.

One of his letters to Evelyn—whom he had been helping to revise his *Numismata*, a 'Discourse on Medals, ancient and modern'—discloses an amusing incident. Bentley's lodgings at St James's were next the Earl of Marlborough's. Bentley wished to annex some rooms overhead, for the better bestowal of certain rare books. Marlborough undertook to plead his cause. The result of this obliging diplomacy was that the future hero of Blenheim got 'the closets' for himself. Bentley now became anxious to build a new library, and Evelyn warmly sympathises with his 'glorious enterprise.' It was, indeed, much needed. The books were so ill-lodged that they could not be properly arranged; Bentley declared that the library was 'not fit to be seen;' and he kept its chief treasure, the Alexandrine MS. of the Greek Bible, at his own rooms in the palace, 'for this very reason, that persons might see it without seeing the library.' The Treasury consented to the proposal for building. But public business prevented the bill coming before Parliament, and the scheme was dropped for the time. Meanwhile Bentley's energy found scope at Cambridge. Since the civil troubles, the University

Press had lapsed into a state which called for reparation. Bentley took an active part in procuring subscriptions for that purpose. He was empowered by the
University to order new founts of type, which were
cast in Holland. Evelyn, in his Diary (Aug. 17, 1696),
alludes to 'that noble presse which my worthy and most
learned friend.. is with greate charge and industrie
erecting now at Cambridge.' In the same year Bentley
took the degree of Doctor in Divinity. On Commence-
ment Sunday (July 5, 1696) he preached before the
University, taking as his text 1 Pet. iii. 15. The
sermon, which is extant, defends Christianity against
deism.

It is natural to ask,—was Bentley yet remarked for
any of those qualities which form the harsher side of his
character in later life? He was now thirty-four. There
is the story of the dinner-party at Bishop Stillingfleet's, at which the guest, who had been sitting next
Bentley, said to the Bishop after dinner, 'My Lord, that
chaplain of yours is certainly a very extraordinary man.'
(Mr. Bentley, like the chaplain in 'Esmond,' had doubtless
conformed to the usage of the time, and retired when the
custards appeared.) 'Yes,' said Stillingfleet, 'had he
but the gift of humility, he would be the most extraordinary man in Europe.' If this has a certain
flavour of concoction, at any rate there is no doubt as to
what Pepys wrote, after reading Boyle's allusion to
Bentley's supposed discourtesy. 'I suspect Mr. Boyle is
in the right; for our friend's learning (which I have a
great value for) wants a little filing.' Against such
hints, there is a noteworthy fact to be set. A letter of
Bentley's to Evelyn, dated Oct. 21, 1697, mentions that
a small group of friends had arranged to meet in the

evenings, once or twice a week, at Bentley's lodgings in St James's. These are the names: John Evelyn, Sir Christopher Wren, John Locke, Isaac Newton. A person with whom such men chose to place themselves in frequent and familiar intercourse must have been distinguished by something else than insolent erudition. But now we must see how Bentley bore himself in the first great crisis of his career.

CHAPTER IV.

THE CONTROVERSY ON THE LETTERS OF PHALARIS.

WILLIAM WOTTON'S *Reflections on Ancient and Modern Learning* (1694) give the best view of a discussion which greatly exercised the wits of the day. 'Soon after the Restauration of King Charles II.,' says Wotton, 'upon the institution of the Royal Society, the comparative excellency of the Old and New Philosophy was eagerly debated in England. But the disputes then managed between Stubbe and Glanvile were rather particular, relating to the Royal Society, than general, relating to knowledge in its utmost extent. In France this controversy has been taken up more at large. The French were not content to argue the point in Philosophy and Mathematicks, but even in Poetry and Oratory too; where the Ancients had the general opinion of the learned· on their side. Monsieur de Fontenelle, the celebrated author of a Book concerning the Plurality of Worlds, began the dispute about six years ago [1688], in a little Discourse annexed to the *Pastorals*.'

Perrault, going further still than Fontenelle, 'in oratory sets the Bishop of Meaux [Bossuet] against Pericles (or rather Thucydides), the Bishop of Nismes [Fléchier]

against Isocrates, F. Bourdaloue against Lysias, Monsieur
Voiture against Pliny, and Monsieur Balzac against
Cicero.   In Poetry likewise he sets Monsieur Boileau
against Horace, Monsieur Corneille and Monsieur Molière
against the Ancient Dramatic Poets.'
    Sir William Temple, in his ' Essay on Ancient and
Modern Learning '—published in 1692, and dedicated to
his own University, *Almae Matri Cantabrigiensi*—was
not less uncompromising in the opposite direction. His
general view is that the Ancients surpassed the Moderns,
not merely in art and literature, but also in every branch
of science, though the records of their science have
perished. ' The Moderns,' Temple adds, ' gather all their
learning out of Books in the Universities.' The Ancients,
on the contrary, travelled with a view to original research, and advanced the limits of knowledge in their
subjects by persistent interviews with reserved specialists
in foreign parts. Thales and Pythagoras are Sir William's
models in this way. ' Thales acquired his knowledge in
Egypt, Phœnicia, Delphos, and Crete ; Pythagoras spent
twenty-two years in Egypt, and twelve years more in
Chaldæa ; and then returned laden with all their stores.'
Temple's performance was translated into French, and
made quite a sensation in the Academy,—receiving,
among other tributes, the disinterested homage of the
Modern Horace.
    Wotton's object was to act as a mediator, and ' give
to every side its just due.' As to ' eloquence and poetry,'
it required some courage (in England) even to hint that
the Moderns had beaten the Ancients. 'It is almost a
heresie in wit, among our poets, to set up any modern
name against Homer or Virgil, Horace or Terence. So
that though here and there one should in Discourse prefer

the writers of the present age, yet scarce any man among us, who sets a value upon his own reputation, will venture to assert it in print.' With regard to science, however, Wotton speaks out, and in a gentle way disposes of the Ancients. He may, in fact, claim the credit of having made a sensible contribution to the discussion. Sir William Temple, 'the ornament of the age,' was no mean antagonist. Wotton must have been glad of a trusty ally, especially on the ground of ancient literature, the strongest part of the enemy's position. Such an ally he found in Bentley. Temple had written thus :—

'It may perhaps be further affirmed, in favour of the Ancients, that the oldest books we have are still in their kind the best. The two most ancient that I know of in prose, among those we call profane authors, are Æsop's Fables and Phalaris's Epistles, both living near the same time, which was that of Cyrus and Pythagoras. As the first has been agreed by all ages since for the greatest master in his kind, and all others of that sort have been but imitations of his original; so I think the Epistles of Phalaris to have more race, more spirit, more force of wit and genius, than any others I have ever seen, either ancient or modern. I know several learned men (or that usually pass for such, under the name of critics) have not esteemed them genuine ; and Politian, with some others, have attributed them to Lucian : but I think he must have little skill in painting that cannot find out this to be an original. Such diversity of passions, upon such variety of actions and passages of life and government ; such freedom of thought, such boldness of expression ; such bounty to his friends, such scorn of his enemies ; such honour of learned men, such esteem of good ; such knowledge of life, such contempt of death ;

with such fierceness of nature and cruelty of revenge, could never be represented but by him that possessed them. And I esteem Lucian to have been no more capable of writing than of acting what Phalaris did. In all one writ you find the scholar or the sophist; in all the other, the tyrant and the commander.'

Mutual admiration and modern journalism have seldom produced a more magnificent advertisement than Sir William Temple had given to this ancient writer. After the slumber, or the doze, of centuries, Phalaris awoke and found himself in demand. The booksellers began to feel an interest in him such as they had never even simulated before.

The 'Epistles of Phalaris' are a collection of a hundred and forty-eight letters,—many of them only a few lines long,—written in 'Attic' Greek of that artificial kind which begins to appear about the time of Augustus. They are first mentioned by a Greek writer, Stobaeus, who flourished about 480 A.D. We know nothing about the exact time at which they were written. On the other hand there is no doubt as to the class of literature which they represent, or the general limits of the period to which they must be assigned. These limits are roughly marked by the first five centuries of the Christian era.

Phalaris, the reputed author of the Letters, is a shadowy figure in the early legends of ancient Sicily. The modern Girgenti, on the south-west coast of the island, preserves the name of Agrigentum, as the Romans called the Greek city of Akragas. Founded early in the sixth century before Christ by a Dorian colony from Gela, Akragas stood on the spacious terraces of a lofty hill. It was a splendid natural stronghold. Steep cliffs were the

city's bulwarks on the south; on the north, a craggy
ridge formed a rampart behind it, and the temple-crowned
citadel, a precipitous rock, towered to a height of twelve
hundred feet above the sea. Story told that Phalaris,
a citizen of Akragas, had contrived to seize the citadel,
and to make himself absolute ruler of the place,—in
Greek phrase, 'tyrant.' He strengthened the city,—then
recently founded,—and was successful in wars upon his
neighbours. At last his own subjects rose against him,
overthrew his power, and put him to death. This latter
event is said to have occurred between 560 and 550 B. C.
Such was the tradition. All that we really know about
Phalaris, however, is that as early as about 500 B. C. his
name had become a proverb for horrible cruelty, not only
in Sicily, but throughout Hellas. Pindar refers to this in
his first Pythian ode (474 B. C.) :—'the kindly worth
of Croesus fades not; but in every land hate follows
the name of *him who burned men in a brazen bull, the
ruthless Phalaris.*'

This habit of slowly roasting objectionable persons in
a brazen bull was the only definite trait which the Greeks
of the classical age associated with Phalaris. And this
is the single fact on which Lucian founds his amusing
piece, in which envoys from Phalaris offer the bull to the
temple of Delphi, and a Delphian casuist urges that it
ought to be accepted. The bull may be seen, portrayed
by the fancy of a modern artist, in the frontispiece to
Charles Boyle's edition of the Letters. The, head of
the brazen animal is uplifted, as if it was bellowing;
one of the tyrant's apparitors is holding up the lid
of a large oblong aperture in the bull's left flank;
two others are hustling in a wretched man, who has
already disappeared, all but his legs. The two servants

wear the peculiar expression of countenance which may
be seen on the faces of persons engaged in packing;
meanwhile another pair of slaves, with more animated
features, are arranging the faggots under the bull, which
are already beginning to blaze cheerfully, so that a gentle
warmth must be felt on the inner surface of the brass,
though it will probably be some minutes yet before it
begins to be uncomfortable. Phalaris is seated on his
throne just behind the bull, in a sort of undress uniform,
with a long round ruler for sceptre in his right hand;
firmness and mildness are so blended in his aspect that it
is impossible not to feel in the presence of a great and
good man; on the left side of the throne, a Polonius is
standing a little in the background, with a look of lively
edification subdued by deference; and in the distance
there is a view of hills and snug farmhouses, suggesting
fair rents and fixity of tenure.

The rather hazy outlines of the old Greek tradition
are filled up by Phalaris himself in the Letters, which
abound with little bits of autobiography. He gives us
to know that he was born,—not at Agrigentum, as
Lucian has it,—but at a place called Astypalaea,
seemingly a town in Crete. He got into trouble there
at an early age, being suspected of aiming at a tyranny,
and was banished, leaving his wife and son behind
him; when he betook himself to Agrigentum, and there
became a farmer of taxes; obtained the management
of a contract for building a temple on the rocky height
above the town; hired troops with the funds thus committed to him; and so made himself master of the place.
Some of the letters are to his wife, his son, and a few of
his particular friends, among whom is the poet Stesichorus.
One or two epistles are addressed to distinguished

strangers, begging them to come and see him in Sicily,—
as to Pythagoras, and Abaris the Hyperborean; and, what
is very curious, the collection gives us the answer sent by
Abaris, which refers not obscurely to the bull, and
declines the invitation of the prince in language more
forcible than polite. Then there are a few letters to
various communities,—the people of Messene, the people
of Tauromenion, and others.

It may be well to give a short specimen or two.
Not a few of the Letters, it should be premised, are
pervaded by a strain of allusion to the bull. Phalaris
was a person of almost morbid sensibility, and if there
was one subject on which he was more alive to innuendo
than another it was this of the bull, and the want of
regard for the feelings of others which his use of it had
been thought to imply. There are moments when he
can no longer suffer in silence, but comes to the point,
as in the following letter to the Athenians [Ep. 122 = 5
(Lennep)]:—

'Your artist Perilaus, Athenians, came to me with
some works of very satisfactory execution; on account of which we gladly received him, and requited
him with worthy gifts, for the sake of his art, and
more particularly for the sake of his native city. Not
long since, however, he made a brazen bull of more than
natural size, and brought it to Akragas. Now we were
delighted to welcome an animal whose labours are
associated with those of man; the effigy appeared a
most proper gift to a prince,—a noble object of art; for
he had not yet disclosed to us the death which lurked
within. But when he opened a door in the flank, and
laid bare

Murder fulfilled of perfect cruelty,
A fate more dire than all imagined death—

then, indeed, after praising him for his skill, we proceeded
to punish him for his inhumanity. We resolved to make
him the first illustration of his own device, since we had
never met with a worse villain than its contriver. So
we put him into the bull, and lit the fire about it,
according to his own directions for the burning. Cruel
was his science; stern the proof to which he brought it.
We did not see the sufferer; we heard not his cries or
lamentations; for the human shrieks that resounded
within came forth to his listening punishers as the
bellowings of a brazen throat.

'Now, Athenians, when I was informed that you
resented the removal of your artist, and were incensed
with me, I felt surprise; and for the present I am
unable to credit the report. If you censure me on the
ground that I did not torment him by a more cruel mode
of death, I reply that no mode more cruel has yet
occurred to me; if, on the other hand, you blame me for
having punished him at all, then your city, which glories
in its humanity, courts the charge of extreme barbarity.
The bull was the work of one Athenian, or of all: but
this will be decided by your disposition towards me....
If you consider the case dispassionately, you will perceive
that I act involuntarily; and that, if Providence decrees
that I must suffer, my lot will be unmerited. Though
my royal power gives me free scope of action, I still
recognise that measures of a harsh tendency are exceptional; and, though I cannot revoke the deeds of the
past, I can confess their gravity. Would, however, that
I had never been compelled to them by a hard necessity!
In that case, no one else would have been named for his
virtues where Phalaris was in company.'

The following letter, addressed by Phalaris to a peevish

critic, shows that consciousness of rectitude had gradually braced the too sensitive mind of the prince [Ep. $66 = 94$ (Lennep)] :—

To Telecleides.

'For reasons best known to yourself, you have repeatedly observed in conversation with my friends that, after the death of Perilaus, the artist of the bull, I ought not to have despatched any other persons by the same mode of torment; since I thus cancel my own merit. Possibly you had in view the result which has actually occurred—viz., that your remarks should be carried to me. Now, as to Perilaus, I do not value myself upon the compliments which I received for having punished him; praise was not my object in assuming that office. As to the other persons, I feel no uneasiness at the misrepresentations to which I am exposed for chastising them. Retribution operates in a sphere apart from good or evil report. Permit me, however, to observe that my reason for correcting the artist was precisely this,—that other persons *were* to be despatched in the bull.... Well, I am now in possession of your views; it is unnecessary for you to trouble other listeners; do but cease to worry yourself and me.'

The slight testiness which appears at the end only confirms Sir William Temple's remark, that here we have to do with a man of affairs, whose time was not to be at the mercy of every idle tattler. After Wotton had published the first edition of his 'Reflections on Ancient and Modern Learning' (1694), Bentley had happened to speak with him of the passage in Temple's Essay which we quoted above. Bentley observed that the Letters of

Phalaris could be proved to be spurious, and that nothing composed by Æsop was extant: opinions which he had formed, and intimated, long before Temple wrote. Wotton then obtained a promise from Bentley that he would give his reasons for these views in a paper to be printed as an appendix to the second edition of the 'Reflections.' But meanwhile an incident occurred which gave a new turn to the matter.

Dr Henry Aldrich, then Dean of Christ Church, had been accustomed to engage the most promising of the younger scholars in the task of editing classical authors, and copies of such editions were usually presented by him to members of the House at the beginning of the year. Temple's essay had attracted attention to the Letters of Phalaris. In 1693 the preparation of a new edition was proposed by the Dean to 'a young Gentleman of great hopes' (as Bentley calls him), the Honourable Charles Boyle, a brother of the Earl of Orrery, and grand-nephew of Robert Boyle, the founder of the Lectures. Charles Boyle was at this time only seventeen. Before coming to Oxford, he had been the private pupil of Dr Gale, the Dean of York (formerly, for a brief space, Greek Professor at Cambridge), of whom he says—'the foundation of all the little knowledge I have in these matters was laid by him, which I gratefully own.' Boyle's scholarship seems to have been quite up to the higher school-standard of that day; he appears to have been bright, clever, and amiable, and was personally much liked at Christ Church. In preparing his Phalaris, he wished to consult a manuscript which was in the King's Library at St James's. He accordingly wrote to his bookseller in London, Mr Thomas Bennet, 'at the Half-Moon in St Paul's Church-yard,' requesting him to

get the manuscript collated. This was apparently in
September, 1693. Bentley had then nothing to do with
the Library. The Royal Patent constituting him Keeper
of His Majesty's Libraries bore date April 12, 1694;
and, owing to delays of form, it was the beginning of
May before he had actual custody of the Library at St
James's. Bennet had already spoken to Bentley (early
in 1694, it seems) about the manuscript of Phalaris; and
Bentley had replied that he would gladly 'help Mr
Boyle to the book.'

Meanwhile Bennet had received urgent applications
from Boyle, and had laid the blame of the delay on
Bentley. As soon as the latter had assumed charge
of the Library (May, 1694), he gave the manuscript
to a person sent for it by Bennet. 'I ordered him,' says
Bentley, ' to tell the collator not to lose any time ; for I
was shortly to go out of town for two months.' This
was afterwards proved by a letter from Gibson, the
person employed as collator. The manuscript remained
in Gibson's hands 'five or six days,' according to Bentley;
and this estimate can scarcely be excessive, for Boyle
himself says merely ' not *nine.*' Bentley was to leave
London for Worcester (to reside two months there) at
five o'clock on a Monday morning towards the end of
May. On the Saturday before, about noon, Bentley
went to Bennet's shop, asked for the manuscript, and
waited while a message was sent to Gibson. Word came
back that Gibson had not finished the collation. Bennet
then begged that the manuscript might be left with him
till Sunday morning, and promised to make the collator
sit up all night. Bentley declined to comply with this
demand ; but said that they might keep the manuscript
till the evening of that day—Saturday. On Saturday

evening it was restored to Bentley. Only forty-eight
letters had then been collated.

As this affair was made a grave charge against
Bentley, it is well to see just what it means. The
business of the collator was to take a printed text
of Phalaris, compare it with the manuscript, and
note those readings in which the manuscript differed
from it. This particular manuscript was, in Bentley's
words, 'as legible as print.' 'I had a mind,' he says,
'for the experiment's sake, to collate the first forty
epistles, which are all that the collator has done. And
I had finished them in an hour and eighteen minutes;
though I made no very great haste. And yet I remarked and set down above fifty various lections, though
the editor has taken notice of one only.' This manuscript
contains only 127 of the 148 letters. At Bentley's rate,
the whole might have been done in about five hours.
Suppose that Bentley worked thrice as fast as Gibson;
the latter would have required fifteen hours. Grant,
further, that Gibson had the manuscript for four days
only, though Boyle's phrase, 'less than nine,' implies
eight. He could still have completed his task by
working less than four hours a day. So utterly groundless was the complaint that Bentley had not allowed
sufficient time for the use of the manuscript.

That, however, was the defence which Bennet
made to his employer. Clearly he had no liking for
the new Librarian who had begun by exacting the dues
of the Royal Library. And he supported it by representing Bentley as unfriendly to Boyle's work. 'The
bookseller once asked me privately,' says Bentley,
'that I would do him the favour to tell my opinion,
if the new edition of Phalaris, then in the press, would

be a vendible book? for he had a concern in the impression, and hoped it would sell well; such a great
character being given of it in [Temple's] Essays as made
it mightily inquired after. I told him, He would be
safe enough, since he was concerned for nothing but
the sale of the book: for the great names of those that
recommended it would get it many buyers. But however,
under the rose, the book was a spurious piece, and deserved not to be spread in the world by another impression.'
Dr William King, a member of Christ Church, and a
'wit,' chanced to be in Bennet's shop one day, and
overheard some remark of Bentley's which he considered
rude towards Boyle. 'After he [Bentley] was gone,'
writes the frank Dr King, 'I told Mr Bennet that he
ought to send Mr Boyle word of it.' Boyle's edition
of Phalaris appeared in January, 1695, with a graceful
dedication to the Dean of Christ Church. The Latin
preface concludes thus :—

'I have collated the letters themselves with two
Bodleian manuscripts from the Cantuar and Selden
collection; I have also procured a collation, as far as
Letter XL., of a manuscript in the Royal Library; the
Librarian, with that courtesy which distinguishes him
[*pro singulari sua humanitate*], refused me the further
use of it. I have not recorded every variation of the
MSS. from the printed texts; to do so would have been
tedious and useless; but, wherever I have departed from
the common reading, my authority will be found in
the notes. This little book is indebted to the printer
for more than usual elegance; it is hoped that the
author's labour may bring it an equal measure of
acceptance.'

Pro singulari sua humanitate : with that courtesy

which distinguishes him : or as Bentley renders it with
grim literalness, ' out of his singular humanity ' ! This,
says Bentley, ' was meant as a lash for me, who had the
honour then and since to serve his Majesty in that office '
(of Librarian) ; and, in fact, the nature of Bentley's
' humanity ' forthwith became a question of the day.

The tone of Boyle's public reference to Bentley was
wholly unjustifiable. Bentley had returned from Worcester
to London some months before Boyle's book was ready,
but no application had been made to him for a further
use of the manuscript, though a few hours would have
finished the collation. Bentley, after his return to
London, spent a fortnight at Oxford, ' conversing,' he
says, ' in the very college where the editors resided ;
not the least whisper there of the manuscript.' It was
on January 26—when the book had been out more
than three weeks—that Bentley chanced to see it for
the first time, ' in the hands of a person of honour to
whom it had been presented ; and the rest of the impression was not yet published. This encouraged me
to write the very same evening to Mr Boyle at Oxford,
and to give him a true information of the whole matter ;
expecting that, upon the receipt of my letter, he would
put a stop to the publication of his book, till he had
altered that passage, and printed the page anew ; which
he might have done in one day, and at the charge of
five shillings. I did not expressly desire him to take
out that passage, and reprint the whole leaf ; that I
thought was too low a submission. But I said enough to
make any person of common justice and ingenuity
[ingenuousness] have owned me thanks for preventing
him from doing a very ill action.' 'After a delay of
two posts,' Boyle replied in terms of which Bentley gives

the substance thus;—'that what I had said in my own
behalf might be true; but that Mr Bennet had represented the thing quite otherwise. If he had had my
account before, he should have considered of it: and
[but?] now that the book was made public, he would
not interpose, but that I might do myself right in
what method I pleased.' On receiving Bentley's explanation, Boyle was clearly bound, if not to withdraw
the offensive passage, at least to stop its circulation
until he had inquired further. And he knew this, as
his own words show. This is his account of his reply
to Bentley:—'That Mr Bennet, whom I employed to
wait on him in my name, gave me such an account of
his reception, that I had reason to apprehend myself af-
fronted: and since I could make no other excuse to my
reader, for not collating the King's MS., but because 'twas
denied me, I thought I cou'd do no less than express
some resentment of that denial. That I shou'd be very
much concern'd if Mr Bennet had dealt so ill with me
as to mislead me in his accounts; *and if that appear'd,
shou'd be ready to take some opportunity of begging his*
[Bentley's] *pardon: and, as I remember, I express'd
myself so, that the Dr might understand I meant to give
him satisfaction as publickly as I had injur'd him. Here
the matter rested, and I thought that Dr Bentley was
satisfied.'*

That is to say, Boyle had offered a public affront to
Bentley, without inquiring whether Bennet's story was
true; Bentley explained that it was untrue; and Boyle
still refused to make any amend, even provisionally.
Bentley was advised by some of his friends to refute
the aspersion: which, indeed, was not merely a charge
of rudeness, but also of failure in his duty as Librarian.

He remained silent. 'Out of a natural aversion to all quarrels and broils, and out of regard to the editor himself, I resolved to take no notice of it, but to let the matter drop.'

But in 1697 Wotton was preparing a second edition of the 'Reflections,' and claimed Bentley's old promise to write something on Æsop and Phalaris. Then, in a great hurry, Bentley wrote an essay on the 'Epistles of Phalaris, Themistocles, Socrates, Euripides, and others; and the Fables of Æsop.' This essay was printed, with a separate title-page, at the end of the new edition of the 'Reflections' (1697). What was he to say about Boyle? 'Upon such an occasion,' he remarks, 'I was plainly obliged to speak of that calumny: for my silence would have been interpreted as good as a confession: especially considering with what industrious malice the story had been spread all over England.' In this he was possibly right: it is not easy to say now. But his mode of self-vindication was certainly not judicious. He ought to have confined himself to a statement of the facts concerning the loan of the manuscript. After doing this, however, he enters upon a hostile review of Boyle's book. Throughout it he speaks in the plural of 'our editors.' He may have had reason to know that Boyle had been assisted; but such a use of the knowledge was unwarrantable.

Boyle's edition was the slight performance of a very young man, and apart from the sentence in the preface, might fairly be regarded as privileged. It contains a short Latin life of Phalaris, based on ancient notices and on the Letters themselves; the Greek text, with a Latin version; and, at the end, some notes. These notes deserve mention only because Bentley was afterwards

accused of having 'pillaged' them. There was a
singular hardihood in this charge. Boyle's notes on the
hundred and forty-eight letters occupy just twelve small
pages. The greater part of them are simply brief para-
phrases intended to bring out the sense of the text.
Three Latin translations of Phalaris then existed; one,
not printed, but easily accessible in manuscript, by
Francesco Accolti of Arezzo (Aretino); a second,
printed by Thomas Kirchmeier, who Hellenized his surname into Naogeorgus (Basel, 1558); and a third, ascribed
to Cujas, which Boyle knew as reissued at Ingolstadt in
1614 for the use of the Jesuit schools. Boyle's version
occasionally coincides with phrases of Aretino or the
Jesuit text: this, however, may well be accident. It is
manifest, however, that his translation was based on that
of Naogeorgus, who is sometimes less elegant, but not
seldom more accurate.

The story of the controversy has usually been told as
if Boyle defended the genuineness of the Letters, while
Bentley impugned it. That is certainly the impression
which any one would derive from Bentley's Dissertation, with its banter of 'our editors and their Sicilian
prince.' Probably it will be new to most persons that
Boyle had never asserted the genuineness of the Letters.
On the contrary, he had expressly stated some reasons for
believing that they were not genuine.

I translate the following from Boyle's Latin preface:—

The reader of these Letters will find less profit in inquiring
who wrote them than pleasure in enjoying the perusal. As to
the authorship, the conflicting opinions of learned men must
be consulted,—perhaps in vain; as to the worth of the book,
the reader can judge best for himself. Lest I disappoint
curiosity, however,—though the controversy does not deserve

keen zeal on either part,—I will briefly explain what seems to
me probable on both sides of the question.

Here he enumerates : (1) some of those who think the
Letters genuine—including Sir W. Temple, whose en-
comium on Phalaris he freely Latinizes : (2) those who
believe the Letters to be the work of Lucian. Here
Boyle gives his reasons—excellent as far as they go—
for holding that Lucian was *not* the author. He then
resumes :—

These are my reasons for not ascribing the letters to
Lucian ; there are other reasons which make me doubt whether
Phalaris can claim the Letters as his own. It was scarcely
possible that Letters written by so distinguished a man, and
in their own kind perfect, should have remained completely
hidden for more than a thousand years : and, as Sicilian
writers always preferred the Dorian dialect, the tyrant of the
Agrigentines (who were Dorians) ought to have used no other.
In the style there is nothing unworthy of a king,—except that
he is too fond of antithesis, and sometimes rather frigid.   I have
also noticed that sometimes (though that may be accidental) the
letters bear names which look as if they had been invented to
suit the contents. As to history, time has robbed us of all certain
knowledge regarding the state of Sicily and its commonwealth,
in that age ; and the recipients of the letters are mostly
obscure, except Stesichorus, Pythagoras, and Abaris ; whose
age agrees with that of Phalaris,—thus affording no hold for
doubt on that ground.   If, however, Diodorus Siculus is right
in saying that Tauromenium, whose citizens our author
addresses, was built and so called after the destruction of
Naxos by the younger Dionysius,—then the claim of Phalaris
is destroyed, and the whole fabric of conjectural ascription falls
to the ground.   This is the sum of what I had to say on my
author,—set forth, indeed, somewhat hastily ; but, if more
learned men have anything to urge against it, I am ready to
hear it.

Boyle wrote this, let it be remembered, before Bentley
had published anything on the subject. Boyle was
strictly justified in saying afterwards, 'I never profess'd
myself a patron of Phalaris;' 'I was not in the least
concern'd to vindicate the Letters.' He defines his own
position with exactness in another place : 'Phalaris was
always a favourite book with me : from the moment I
knew it, I wish'd it might prove an original : I had now
and then, indeed, some suspicions that 'twas not genuine;
but I lov'd him so much more than I suspected him, that
I wou'd not suffer myself to dwell long upon 'em.   To
be sincere, the opinion, or mistake, if you will, was so
pleasing that I was somewhat afraid of being undeceiv'd.'
It was Sir William Temple, not Boyle, who was committed to the view that the Letters were genuine.

We shall speak of Bentley's Dissertation in its second
and mature form.   The first rough draft, in Wotton's
book, is a rapid argument, with just enough illustration
to make each topic clear.   It had been very hastily
written.   That Boyle and his friends should have been
angry, can surprise no one.   Bentley, in rebutting a
calumny, had become a rough assailant.   A reply came
out in January, 1696.   It was entitled, 'Dr Bentley's
Dissertations on the Epistles of Phalaris and the Fables
of Æsop, examin'd by the Honourable Charles Boyle,
Esq.'   The motto was taken from Roscommon's 'Essay
of Translated Verse :'

Remember Milo's end ;
Wedg'd in that Timber, which he strove to rend.

The piece is clever and effective.   'Soon after Dr
Bentley's Dissertation came out,' Boyle says in the
preface, ' I was call'd away into Ireland, to attend the
Parliament there.   The publick business, and my own

private affairs, detain'd me a great while in that kingdom;
else the world should have had a much earlier account of
him and his performance.' Boyle explains that he had
edited the Letters 'rather as one that wish'd well to
learning than profess'd it.' His motive for replying to
Bentley's attack is ' the publick affront' of being charged
with setting his name to a book which was not his own.
No one had helped him in it,—except one friend who had
been his adviser 'upon any difficulty,' and had also
consulted 'some books' for him 'in the Oxford Libraries.'
As to the Letters, he had neither asserted nor denied
their genuineness. He is sorry to have been the occasion
of bringing such a storm on the head of Sir William
Temple. He regrets, too, that Bentley should have
extended his aspersions to Christ Church. Then comes
an onslaught on Bentley's essay and a defence of Boyle's
book. 'A Short Account of Dr Bentley by way of
Index' was appended to the second edition. This is an
index to the preceding 266 pages, under such heads as
these :—' Dr Bentley's civil usage of Mr Boyle; His
singular humanity to Mr Boyle; His elegant Similes; His
clean and gentile Metaphors; His old Sayings and Proverbs; His Collection of Asinine Proverbs; His extraordinary talent at Drollery; His dogmatical air; His
Ingenuity in transcribing and plundering Notes and
Prefaces of Mr Boyle [here follows a list of other victims].
His modesty and decency in contradicting Great Men
[here follows a list of the persons contradicted, ending
with Everybody].'

This, we know, was a joint performance. Francis
Atterbury, afterwards Bishop of Rochester, was then
thirty-six : George Smalridge was a year younger. Both
were already distinguished at Oxford. Atterbury, in a

letter to Boyle, says with reference to this piece : 'in
writing more than half of the book, in reviewing a good
part of the rest, in transcribing the whole and attending
the press half a year of my life has passed away.'
Smalridge is supposed to have contributed a playful proof
that Bentley did not write his own essay. This is a
parody of Bentley's arguments about Phalaris, partly
woven with his own words and phrases. This sham
Bentley—urges the critic—'is a perfect Dorian in his
language, in his thoughts, and in his breeding.' It is vain
to plead that 'he was born in some Village remote from
Town, and bred among the Peasantry while young.'
The real Bentley had been 'a Member of one University,
and a Sojourner in the other; a Chaplain in Ordinary to
the King, and a Tutor in extraordinary to a Young
Gentleman:' such a man must surely have written
Attic; he must 'have quitted his Old Country Dialect
for that of a Londoner, a Gentleman, and a Scholar.'
Then the sham Bentley is 'a Fierce and Angry Writer;
and One, who when he thinks he has an advantage over
another Man, gives him no Quarter.' But the real
Bentley says in his Letter to Dr Mill, 'it is not in my
nature to trample upon the Prostrate.' The real Bentley
was 'much vers'd in the Learned Languages.' This
pseudo-Bentley shows 'that he was not only a perfect
Stranger to the best Classic Authors, but that he wanted
that Light which any Ordinary Dictionary would have
afforded him.' The pages on Æsop may have been
chiefly due to Anthony Alsop, a young Student of
Christ Church, who edited the Fables in that year (1698).
The 'very deserving gentleman' to whom Boyle refers
as his assistant appears to have been John Freind, whose
brother Robert (both were Students of Christ Church) is

also believed to have helped. Some of the insults to
Bentley are very gross. Thus it is hinted, twice over,
that his further compliance in the matter of the manuscript might have been purchased by a fee. This is the
only thing in the piece which Bentley noticed with a
word of serious reproof.

The book gives us some curious glimpses of the
way in which critical studies were then viewed by Persons of Honour. 'Begging the Dr's pardon,' says Boyle,
'I take *Index-hunting* after Words and Phrases to be,
next after *Anagrams* and *Acrosticks*, the lowest Diversion
a Man can betake himself to.' Boyle is apprehensive lest
'worthy Men, who know so well how to employ their
hours, should be diverted from the pursuit of Useful
Knowledge into such trivial Enquiries as these :' and he
shrinks from being suspected of having 'thrown away any
considerable part of his life on so trifling a subject.' He
need not have felt much uneasiness.

However small Boyle's share in this book may
have been, it is right to observe that there is an almost
ludicrous exaggeration in the popular way of telling the
story, as if all Christ Church, or all Oxford, had been
in a league to annihilate Bentley. The joint book
was written by a group of clever friends who represented only themselves. Rymer, indeed, says, 'Dr Aldrich, no doubt, was at the head of them, and smoaked
and punned plentifully on this occasion.' But this was
a mistake. The 'Short Review' published anonymously in 1701 (the author was Atterbury) says expressly :—'That an answer was preparing, he [the Dean
of Christ Church] knew nothing of till 'twas publick
talk, and he never saw a line of the *Examination* but in
Print.'

In the preface to Anthony Alsop's Æsop—another of
the Christ Church editions, which came out, before Boyle's
book, early in 1698—our hero is mentioned as 'a certain
Bentley, diligent enough in turning over lexicons;' and
his behaviour about the manuscript is indicated by a
Latin version of 'The Dog in the Manger.' The wearied
ox, coming home to dinner, is driven from his hay by
the snarling usurper, and remonstrates warmly; when
the dog replies, 'You call me currish; if foreigners are
any judges, there is not a hound alive that approaches
me in humanity.' To whom the ox: 'Is this your
singular humanity, to refuse me the food that you will
not and cannot enjoy yourself?'

At last 'Boyle against Bentley' came out (1698). Its
success was enormous. A second edition was called for
in a few months. A third edition followed in the next
year. Forty-six years later, when both the combatants
were dead, it was still thought worth while to publish
a fourth edition.

Temple lost no time in pronouncing. In March, just
after the book appeared, he writes:—'The compass
and application of so much learning, the strength and
pertinence of his (Boyle's) arguments, the candour of
his relations, in return to such foul-mouthed raillery,
the pleasant turns of wit, and the easiness of style,
are in my opinion as extraordinary as the contrary
of these all appear to be in what the Doctor and his
friend [Wotton] have written.' Hard as this is on
Bentley, it is harder still on poor Wotton, who had
been elaborately civil to Temple. Garth published
his *Dispensary* in 1699, with that luckless couplet,—
meant, says Noble, 'to please his brother wits at
Button's:'—

> So diamonds take a lustre from their foil,
> And to a Bentley 'tis we owe a Boyle.

John Milner, formerly Vicar of Leeds, had, as a non-juror, lost his preferments at the Revolution, and was then living at St John's College, Cambridge. In his 'View of the Dissertation' (1698) he proposes 'to manifest the incertitude of heathen chronology,' and takes part against Bentley. According to Eustace Budgell, a caricature was published at Cambridge, in which Phalaris was consigning Bentley to the bull, while the Doctor exclaimed, 'I would rather be roasted than boyled.' Rymer, in his 'Essay on Critical and Curious Learning' (1698), blames both parties. As to the question at issue, he argues that 'curious' learning is all very well in its way, but should not be carried too far. On Boyle's critique Rymer makes a shrewd remark : 'There is such a profusion of wit all along, and such variety of points and raillery, that every man seems to have thrown in a repartee or so in his turn.' Mr Cole (of Magdalen College, Oxford) compared it to 'a Cheddar cheese, made of all the milk of the parish.'

In short, 'society' had declared against Bentley, and the men of letters almost unanimously agreed with it. While other acquaintances were turning their backs, Evelyn stood loyal. That was the state of things in 1698. Bentley remained calm. A friend who met him one day urged him not to lose heart. 'Indeed,' he replied, 'I am in no pain about the matter ; for it is a maxim with me that no man was ever written out of reputation but by himself.' Meanwhile he was preparing a reply.

CHAPTER V.

WE have seen that Bentley's essay in Wotton's book had been a hasty production. 'I drew up that dissertation,' he says, 'in the spare hours of a few weeks; and while the Printer was employed about one leaf, the other was amaking.' He now set to work to revise and enlarge it. He began his task about March, 1698—soon after Boyle's pamphlet appeared—but was interrupted in it by the two months of his residence at Worcester, from the end of May to the end of July. It was finished towards the close of 1698. The time employed upon it had thus been about seven and a half months, not free from other and urgent duties. It was published early in 1699. Let us clearly apprehend the point at issue. Boyle did not assert that the Letters of Phalaris were genuine; but he denied that Bentley had yet proved them to be spurious.

After a detailed refutation of the personal charges against him, Bentley comes to the Letters of Phalaris. First he takes the flagrant anachronisms. The Letters mention towns which, at the supposed date, were not built, or bore other names. Phalaris presents his physician with the ware of a potter named Thericles,—much as if

Oliver Cromwell were found dispensing the masterpieces of Wedgwood. Phalaris quotes books which had not been written; nay, he is familiar with forms of literature which had not been created. Though a Dorian, he writes to his familiar friends in Attic, and in a species of false Attic which did not exist for five centuries after he was dead. Farmer of the taxes though he had been, he has no idea of values in the ordinary currency of his own country. Thus he complains that the hostile community of Catana had made a successful raid on his principality, and had robbed him of no less a sum than seven talents. Again he mentions with some complacency that he has bestowed the munificent dower of five talents on a lady of distinction. According to the Sicilian standard, the loss of the prince would have amounted to twelve shillings and seven pence, while the noble bride would have received nine shillings. The occasions of the letters, too, are often singular. A Syracusan sends his brother to Akragas, a distance of a hundred miles, with a request that Phalaris would send a messenger to Stesichorus (another hundred miles or so), and beg that poet to write a copy of verses on the Syracusan's deceased wife. 'This,' says Bentley, 'is a scene of putid and senseless formality.' Then Phalaris (who brags in one of the letters that Pythagoras had stayed five months with him) says to Stesichorus, '*pray* do not mention me in your poems.' 'This,' says Bentley, 'was a sly fetch of our sophist, to prevent so shrewd an objection from Stesichorus's silence as to any friendship at all with him.' But supposing Phalaris had really been so modest— Bentley adds,—still, Stesichorus was a man of the world. The poet would have known 'that those sort of requests are but a modest simulation, and a disobedience would have been easily pardoned.' Again, these Letters are not mentioned by any writer before the fifth century of our era, and it is clear that the ancients did not know them. Thus, in the Letters, Phalaris displays the greatest solicitude for the education of his son Paurolas, and writes to the young man in terms which would do credit to the best of fathers. But in Aristotle's time there was a tradition which placed the parental conduct of Phalaris in another light. It alleged, in fact, that, while this boy was still of a tender age, the prince had caused him to be served up at table: but how, asks Bentley,— supposing the Letters to be genuine—'could he eat his son while he was an infant?' It is true, the works of some writers in the early Christian centuries (Phædrus, Paterculus, Lactantius) are not mentioned till long after their death. But the interval was one during which the Western world was lapsing into barbarism. The supposed epoch of Phalaris was followed by 'the greatest and longest reign of learning that the world has yet seen:' and yet his Letters remain hidden for a thousand years. 'Take them in the whole bulk, they are a fardle of commonplaces, without any life or spirit from action and circumstance. Do but cast your eye upon Cicero's letters, or any statesman's, as Phalaris was; what lively characters of men there! what descriptions of place! what notifications of time! what particularity of circumstances! what multiplicity of designs and events! When you return to these again, you feel, by the emptiness and deadness of them, that you converse with some dreaming pedant with his elbow on his desk; not with an active, ambitious tyrant, with his hand on his sword, commanding a million of subjects.'

Bentley's incidental discussions of several topics are so

many concise monographs, each complete in itself, each
exhaustive within its own limits, and each, at the same
time, filling its due place in the economy of the whole.
Such are the essays on the age of Pythagoras, on the
beginnings of Greek Tragedy, on anapæstic verse, on the
coinage of Sicily. In the last-named subject, it might
have appeared almost impossible that a writer of Bentley's
time should have made any near approximation to
correctness. He had not such material aids as are
afforded by the Sicilian coins which we now possess,—
without which the statements of ancient writers would
appear involved in hopeless contradiction. I am
glad, therefore, to quote an estimate of Bentley's
work in this department by a master of numismatic
science. Mr Barclay Head writes :—'Speaking generally, Bentley's results are surprisingly accurate. I
think I may safely say that putting aside what was to
have been done within the last fifty years, Bentley's essay
stands alone. Even Eckhel, in his 'Doctrina numorum'
(1790), has nothing to compare with it.' Again, Bentley's
range and grasp of knowledge are strikingly seen in
critical remarks of general bearing which are drawn from
him by the course of the discussion. Thus at the outset
he gives in a few words a broad view of the origin and
growth of literary forgery in the ancient world. In the
last two centuries before Christ, when there was a keen
rivalry between the libraries of Pergamus and Alexandria,
the copiers of manuscripts began the practice of inscribing
them with the names of great writers, in order that they
might fetch higher prices. Thus far, the motive of
falsification was simply mercenary. But presently a
different cause began to swell the number of spurious
works. It was a favourite exercise of rhetoric, in the

early period of the Empire, to compose speeches or letters
in the name and character of some famous person. At
first such exercises would, of course, make no pretence
of being anything more. But, as the art was developed,
'some of the Greek Sophists had the success and
satisfaction to see their essays in that kind pass with some
readers for the genuine works of those they endeavoured
to express. This, no doubt, was great content and joy to
them; being as full a testimony of their skill in imitation,
as the birds gave to the painter when they pecked at his
grapes.' [1] Some of them, indeed, candidly confessed the
trick. 'But most of them took the other way, and,
concealing their own names, put off their copies for
originals; preferring that silent pride and fraudulent
pleasure, though it was to die with them, before an
honest commendation from posterity for being good
imitators.' [2] And hence such Letters as those of Phalaris.

Dr Aldrich had lately dedicated his Logic to Charles
Boyle. Bentley makes a characteristic use of this
circumstance. 'If his new System of Logic teaches him
such arguments,' says Bentley, 'I'll be content with the
old ones.' The whole Dissertation, in fact, is a re-
morseless syllogism. But Bentley is more than a sound
reasoner. He shows in a high degree the faculties which
go to make debating power. He is frequently successful
in the useful art of turning the tables. Alluding to
his opponent's mock proof that 'Dr Bentley could not be
the author of the Dissertation,' he remarks that Boyle's
Examination is open to a like doubt in good earnest, if
we are to argue 'from the variety of styles in it, from its
contradictions to his edition of Phalaris, from its contradictions to itself, from its contradictions to Mr B.'s
character and to his title of honourable.' Boyle had said

of Bentley, 'the man that writ this must have been fast
asleep, for else he could never have talked so wildly.'
Bentley replies, 'I hear a greater paradox talked of
abroad; that not the "wild" only, but the best, part of
the Examiner's book may possibly have been written
while he was fast asleep.'

He is often neat, too, in exploding logical fallacies.
Boyle argued that, as Diodorus gives two different dates
for the founding of Tauromenium, neither can be trusted.
Bentley rejoins: 'One man told me in company that the
Examiner was twenty-four years old; and another said,
twenty-five. Now, these two stories contradict one another, and neither can be depended on; we are at liberty,
therefore, to believe him a person of about fifty years of
age.' Boyle had taken refuge in a desperate suggestion
that people might have been called 'Tauromenites' from a
river Tauromenius, before there was a city Tauromenium.
'Now,' says Bentley, 'if the Tauromenites were a sort of
fish, this argument drawn from the river would be of
great force.' Boyle had argued that a Greek phrase was
not poetical because each of the two words forming it was
common. Bentley quotes from Lucretius—

>   Luna dies, et nox, et noctis signa severa.

Is not every word common? And is the total effect pro-
saic? Bentley's retort is a mere quibble, turning on the
ambiguity of 'common' as meaning either 'vulgar' or
'simple,'—but illustrates his readiness. Once,—as if in
contempt for his adversary's understanding,—he has
indulged in a notable sophism. Boyle had argued
that the *name* 'tragedy' cannot have existed before the
thing. Bentley rejoins:—''tis a proposition false in itself
that things themselves must be, before the names by

which they are called. For we have many new
tunes in music made every day, which never existed
before ; yet several of them are called by *names* that were
formerly in use ; and perhaps the tune of Chevy Chase,
though it be of famous antiquity, is a little younger than
the name of the chase itself. And I humbly conceive
that Mr Hobbes's book, which he called the *Leviathan*,
is not quite as ancient as its name is in Hebrew.'
But the 'name' of which Boyle spoke was descriptive,
not merely appellative. Bentley's reasoning would have
been relevant only if Boyle had argued that, since a
tragedy is called the 'Agamemnon,' Tragedy must have
existed before Agamemnon lived.

As to the English style of the Dissertation, the
Boyle party had expressed their opinion pretty freely
when the first draft of it had appeared in Wotton's
book. They complained that, when Bentley 'had occasion
to express himself in Terms of Archness and Waggery,'
he descended to 'low and mean Ways of Speech.' 'The
familiar expressions of *taking one tripping,—coming
off with a whole skin,—minding his hits,—a friend at a
pinch,—going to blows,—setting horses together,—*and
going to pot ; with others borrow'd from the Sports and
Employments of the Country ; shew our Author to have
been accustom'd to another sort of Exercise than that of
the Schools.' Alluding to the painful fate which was
said to have overtaken the mother of Phalaris, Bentley
particularly shocked his critics by the phrase, '*Roasting
the Old Woman ;*' and, in a similar strain of rustic levity
he had described the parent of Euripides as '*Mother Clito
the Herbwoman.*' Dr King, of Christ Church, (who, it
will be remembered, had meddled in the manuscript
affair,) had written an account of a journey to London ;

wherein he relates that, on his asking concerning the ales
at a certain inn, the host answered 'that he had a
thousand such sort of liquors, as humtie dumtie, three-
threads, four-threads, old Pharoah [sic], knockdown, hug-
metee,' &c. Playfully referring to this passage, Bentley
says (speaking of a wild assertion), 'A man must be
dosed with Humty-dumty that could talk so incon-
sistently :' and again, speaking of Dr King's statements,
'If he comes with more testimonies of his Bookseller or
his Humty-dumty acquaintance, I shall take those for
no answer.' Worst of all, this familiar style was used
towards Phalaris himself and his defenders. Speaking of
the Greek rhetoricians, Bentley announces that his
design is 'to pull off the disguise from those little
Pedants that have so long stalkt about in the Apparel
of Heroes.' The work of Boyle and his assistants is
thus characterised : 'Here are your Work-men to mend
an author; as bungling Tinkers do old kettles; there
was but one hole in the text before they meddled with it,
but they leave it with two.'

Not a soothing style this, nor one to be recommended
for imitation. But what vigour there is in some of the
phrases that Bentley strikes out at a red heat! They
ought to have made inquiries 'before they ventur'd to
Print,—*which is a sword in the hand of a Child.*' 'He
gives us some shining metaphors, and a polished period
or two; but, for the matter of it, it is *some common
and obvious thought dressed and curled in the beauish
way.*' Speaking of work which Bishop Pearson had
left unfinished : 'though it has not passed the last hand
of the author, yet it's every way worthy of him; and
the *very dust of his writings is gold.*' And here,—
as Bentley was charged in this controversy with such

boundless arrogance, and such 'indecency in contradicting
great men,'—let us note his tone in the Dissertation
towards eminent men then living or lately dead.   Nothing
could be more becoming, more worthy of his own genius,
than the warm, often glowing, terms in which he speaks
of such men as Selden, Pearson, Lloyd, Stillingfleet,
Spanheim,—in a word, of almost all the distinguished
scholars whom he has occasion to name.   Dodwell, who
was ranged against him, is treated with scrupulous
courtesy and fairness.   Joshua Barnes, whose own conduct to Bentley had been remarkably bad, could scarcely
be described more indulgently than in these words,—
'one of a singular industry and a most diffuse reading.'
Those were precisely the two things which could truly be
said in praise of Barnes, and it would not have been
easy to find a third.

Hallam characterises the style of the Dissertation as
'rapid, concise, amusing, and superior to Boyle in that
which he had chiefly to boast, a sarcastic wit.'   It may
be questioned how far 'wit,' in its special modern sense,
was a distinguishing trait on either side of this controversy.   The chief weapons of the Boyle alliance were
rather derision and invective.   Bentley's sarcasm is always
powerful and often keen; but the finer quality of wit,
though seen in some touches, can hardly be said to
pervade the Dissertation.   As to the humour, that is
unquestionable.   There is so far an unconscious element
in it, that its effect on the reader is partly due to
Bentley's tremendous and unflagging earnestness in
heaping up one absurdity upon another.   This cumulative
humour belongs to the essay as a whole; as Bentley
marches on triumphantly from one exposure to another,
our sense of the ludicrous is constantly rising.   But it

can be seen on a smaller scale too. For instance, one of Boyle's grievances was that Bentley had indirectly called him an ass. In Bentley's words :—'By the help, he says, of a Greek proverb, I call him a downright ass. After I had censured a passage of Mr Boyle's translation that has no affinity with the original, *This puts me in mind*, said I, *of the old Greek proverb, that Leucon carries one thing, and his Ass quite another.* Where the Ass is manifestly spoken of the Sophist [the real author of the Letters,] whom I had before represented as *an Ass under a Lion's skin.* And if Mr B. has such a dearness for his Phalaris that he'll change places with him there, how can I help it? I can only protest that I put him into Leucon's place ; and if he will needs compliment himself out of it, *"I must leave the two friends to the pleasure of their mutual civilities."* [Boyle's own words about Bentley and Wotton.] But this was not all : Boyle had accused Bentley of comparing him to *Lucian's* ass. Now this, says Bentley, 'were it true, would be no coarse compliment, but a very obliging one. For Lucian's Ass was a very intelligent and ingenious Ass, and had more sense than any of his Riders; he was no other than Lucian himself in the shape of an ass, and had a better talent at kicking and bantering than ever the Examiner will have, though it seems to be his chief one.' 'But is this Mr B.'s way of interpreting similitudes?...If I liken an ill critic to a bungling Tinker, that makes two holes while he mends one; must I be charged with calling him Tinker? At this rate Homer will call his heroes Wolves, Boars, Dogs, and Bulls. And when Horace has this comparison about himself,

Demitto auriculas, ut iniquae mentis asellus,

Mr B. may tell him that he calls himself downright
ass. But he must be put in mind of the English proverb,
that similitudes, even when they are taken from asses, do
not walk upon all four.' Swift,—alluding to the trans-
ference of the Letters from Phalaris to their real
source,—called Bentley that 'great rectifier of saddles.'
Bentley might have replied that he could rectify
panniers too.

It would be a mistake to regard Bentley's Dissertation
as if its distinctive merit had consisted in demonstrating
the Letters of Phalaris to be spurious. That was by
no means Bentley's own view. The spuriousness of
these Letters, he felt from the first, was patent. He had
given (in Wotton's book) a few of the most striking
proofs of this : and he had been attacked. Now he was
showing, in self-defence, that his proofs not only held
good, but had deep and solid foundations. Others before
him had suspected that the letters were forgeries, and he
would have scorned to take the smallest credit for seeing
what was so plain. He was the first to give sufficient
reasons for his belief : but he did not care, and did not
pretend, to give all the reasons that might be adduced.
Indeed, any careful reader of the Letters can remark
several proofs of spuriousness. on which Bentley has not
touched. For instance, it could be shown that the
fictitious proper names are post-classical ; that the forger
was acquainted with Thucydides ; and that he had read
the *Theaetetus* of Plato. But Bentley had done more
than enough for his purpose. The glory of his treatise
was not that it established his conclusion, but that it
disclosed that broad and massive structure of learning
upon which his conclusion rested. 'The only book that
I have writ upon my own account,' he says, 'is this

present answer to Mr B.'s objections; and I assure him
I set no great price upon 't; the errors that it refutes
are so many, so gross and palpable, that I shall never be
very proud of the victory.' At the same time, he justly
refutes the assertion of his adversaries that the point at
issue was of no moment. Bentley replies :—'That the
single point whether Phalaris be genuine or no is of no
small importance to learning, the very learned Mr Dodwell
is a sufficient evidence; who, espousing Phalaris for a
true author, has endeavoured by that means to make a
great innovation in the ancient chronology. To under-
value this dispute about Phalaris because it does not suit
to one's own studies, is to quarrel with a circle because it
is not a square.'

A curious fatality attended on Bentley's adversaries in this controversy. While they dealt thrusts
at points where he was invulnerable, they missed all the
chinks in his armour except a statement limiting too
narrowly the use of two Greek verbs, and his identi-
fication of 'Alba Graeca' with Buda instead of Belgrade.
Small and few, indeed, these chinks were. It would
have been a petty, but fair, triumph for his opponents,
if they had perceived that, in correcting a passage of
Aristophanes, he had left a false quantity. They might
have shown that a passage in Diodorus had led him
into an error regarding Attic chronology during
the reign of the Thirty Tyrants. They might have
exulted in the fact that an emendation which he
proposed in Isaeus rested on a confusion between two
different classes of choruses; that he had certainly
misconstrued a passage in the life of Pythagoras by
Iamblichus; that the 'Minos,' on which he relies as
Plato's work, was spurious; that, in one of the Letters

of Phalaris, he had defended a false reading by false
grammar. They could have shown that Bentley was
demonstrably wrong in asserting that no writings, bearing
the name of Æsop, were extant in the time of Aristophanes; also in stating that the Fable of 'The Two
Boys' had not come down to the modern world: it
was, in fact, very near them,—safe in a manuscript
at the Bodleian Library. Even the discussion on Za-
leucus escaped: its weak points were first brought out
by later critics—Warburton, Salter, Gibbon. Had such
blemishes been ten times more numerous, they would
not have affected the worth of the book: but, such as
they were, they were just of the kind which small
detractors delight to magnify. In one place Bentley
accuses Boyle of having adopted a wrong reading
in one of the Letters, and thereby made nonsense
of the passage. Now, Boyle's reading, though not the
best, happens to be capable of yielding the very sense
which Bentley required. Yet even this Boyle and his
friends did not discover.

How was the Dissertation received? According to the
popular account, no sooner had Bentley blown his mighty
blast, than the walls of the hostile fortress fell flat. The
victory was immediate, the applause universal, the foe's
ruin overwhelming. Tyrwhitt, in his *Babrius*—published
long after Bentley's death—is seeking to explain why
Bentley never revised the remarks on Æsop, which he had
published in Wotton's book. 'Content with having
prostrated his adversaries with the second Dissertation
on Phalaris, as by a thunderbolt, he withdrew in scorn
from the uneven fight.'

Let us see what the evidence is. Just as the great
Dissertation appeared, Boyle's friends published 'A short

Account of Dr Bentley's Humanity and Justice.' It is
conceived in a rancorous spirit; Bentley is accused of
having plundered, in his Fragments of Callimachus, some
papers which Thomas Stanley, the editor of Aeschylus,
left unpublished at his death; and Bentley's conduct to
Boyle about the manuscript is set forth as related by the
bookseller, Mr Bennet. Now, in John Locke's correspondence, I find a letter to him from Thomas Burnet,
formerly a Fellow of Christ's College, Cambridge, and
then Master of Charterhouse,—author of a fantastic
book on the geological history of the earth (*Telluris
Theoria Sacra*). The date is March 19, 1699. Bentley had read part of his preface to Burnet before it
was published. Burnet had now read the whole, and a
great part of the Dissertation itself; also the newly
published 'Short Account.' He is now disposed to believe
Bennet's version. 'I do profess upon second thoughts...
that his story seemeth the more likely, if not the most
true, of the two.' As to the letters of Phalaris, he is
aware that some great scholars are with Bentley. 'But
I doubt not,' he adds, 'that a greater number will be of
another sentiment, who would not be thought to be of the
unlearned tribe.' That, we may be sure, was what
many people were saying in London. A defence of
Bentley against the 'Short Account,' which came out at
this time, has been ascribed to a Fellow of Magdalen
College, Oxford,—Solomon Whately, the first translator
of Phalaris into English.

The Boyle party had addressed themselves to the wits
and the town. Bentley's work had plenty of qualities
which could be appreciated in that quarter: but its
peculiar strength lay in things of which few persons could
judge. These few were at once convinced by it: and

their authority helped to convince the inner circles of
students. But the Boyle party still had on their side
all those who, regarding the contest as essentially an
affair of style, preferred Boyle's style to Bentley's. This
number would include the rank and file of fashion and its
dependents,—the persons who wrote dedications, and the
patrons in whose antechambers they waited. Most of
them would be genuinely unconscious how good Bentley's answer was, and their prepossessions would set
strongly the other way. So, while Bentley had persuaded
the scholars, it would still be the tone of a large and influential world to say that, though the pedant might have
brought cumbrous proofs of a few trivial points, Boyle
had won a signal victory in 'wit, taste, and breeding.'

Swift's 'Battle of the Books' was begun when he was
living with Sir William Temple at Moor Park in 1697.
It was suggested by a French satire,—Coutray's *Histoire
Poétique de la guerre nouvellement déclarée entre les
anciens et les modernes*,—and referred to Bentley's *first*
dissertation, which had just appeared. Temple was feeling
sore, and Swift wished to please him. But its circulation
was only private until it was published with the 'Tale of a
Tub' in 1704. Temple had then been dead five years.
If Bentley's victory had then been universally recognised
as crushing, Swift would have been running the risk of
turning the laugh against himself; and no man, so fond
of wounding, liked that less. In the 'Battle of the Books,'
Boyle is Achilles, clad in armour wrought by the gods.
The character ascribed to Bentley and Wotton is expressed
in the Homeric similes which adorn the grand battle at
the end. 'As a Woman in a little House, that gets a
painful livelihood by spinning; if chance her Geese be
scattered o'er the Common, she courses round the plain

from side to side, compelling, here and there, the stragglers
to the flock ; they cackle loud, and flutter o'er the cham-
pain : so Boyle pursued, so fled this Pair of Friends......
As when a skilful Cook has truss'd a brace of Woodcocks,
he, with iron Skewer, pierces the tender sides of both,
their legs and wings close pinion'd to their ribs; so was this
Pair of Friends transfix'd, till down they fell, join'd in their
lives, join'd in their deaths ; so closely join'd that Charon
would mistake them both for one, and waft them over Styx
for half his fare.' When this was first published, Bentley's
second Dissertation had been five years before the public.

Against this satire—so purely popular that it lost
nothing by being whetted on the wrong edge—we must set
two pieces of contemporary evidence to Bentley's immediate success with his own limited audience. In discussing
the age of Pythagoras, he had said : 'I do not pretend
to pass my own judgment, or to determine positively on
either side; but I submit the whole to the censure of such
readers as are well versed in ancient learning ; and particularly to that incomparable historian and chronologer, the
Right Reverend the Bishop of Coventry and Litchfield.'
In the same year (1699) Dr Lloyd responded by publishing his views on the question, prefaced by a dedicatory
epistle to Bentley. The other testimony is of a different
kind, but not less significant. 'A Short Review' of the
controversy appeared in 1701. It was anonymous.
Dyce says that a friend of his possessed a copy in which
an early eighteenth century hand had written, 'by Dr
Atterbury.' The internal evidence leaves no doubt of
this. I may notice one indication of it, which does not
appear to have been remarked. We have seen that the
'Examination' of Bentley's first essay was edited, and in
great part written, by Atterbury. This ends with these

words :—'I fancy that the reader will be glad to have...
the Dr's Picture in Miniature,' rather 'than that it shou'd
be again drawn out *at full length*.' The 'picture in
miniature' is the 'Index' already mentioned above. Now
the 'Short Review' ends with 'the Dr's Advantagious
Character of himself *at full length*.' The writer of this
'Character' is clearly going back on his own footsteps : and
that writer can be no other than Atterbury. He is very
angry, and intensely bitter. He hints that Whig interest
has bolstered up Bentley against Tory opponents. With
almost incredible violence, he accuses Bentley of 'lying,
stealing, and prevaricating' (p. 12). He contrasts the
character of a 'Critic' with that of a 'Gentleman.' Stress
is laid on the imputation that Bentley had attacked not
Boyle alone, but also the illustrious society in which
Boyle had been educated. The members of that
society (Atterbury remarks), are not cut all alike as
Bushels are by Winchester-measure : 'But they are men
of different Talents, Principles, Humours and Interests,
who are seldom or never united save when some unreason-
able oppression from abroad fastens them together, and
consequently whatever ill is said of all of them is falsely
said of many of them.' 'To answer the reflexion of a private Gentleman with a general abuse of the Society he
belong'd to, is the manners of a dirty Boy upon a Country-
Green.' It will not avail Bentley that his friends 'style
him a Living Library, a Walking Dictionary, and a Con-
stellation of Criticism.' A solitary gleam of humour
varies this strain. Some wiseacre had suggested that the
Letters of Phalaris might corrupt the crowned heads of
Europe, if kings should take up the Agrigentine
tyrant as Alexander the Great took up Homer, and put
him under their pillows at night. 'I objected'—says the

author of the 'Short Review'—'that now, since the advancement of Learning and Civility in the world, Princes
were more refined, and would be ashamed of such acts of
Barbarity as Phalaris was guilty of in a ruder age.' But
the alarmist stuck to his point; urging that 'his Czarish
Majesty' (Peter the Great, then in the twelfth year of
his reign) might have met with the Letters of Phalaris in
his travels, and that 'his curiosity might have led him to
make a Brazen Bull, when he came home, to burn his
Rebells in.' The piece ends by renewing the charge of
plagiarism against Bentley. Considering that the second
Dissertation had now been out two years, this is a
curiosity of literature :—'*Common Pilferers will still go
on in their trade, even after they have suffer'd for it.*'

But, when Bentley's Dissertation had been published
for half-a-century, surely there can have been no longer
any doubt as to the completeness of his victory? We
shall see. In 1749, seven years after Bentley's death, an
English Translation of the Letters of Phalaris was
published by Thomas Francklin. He had been educated
at Westminster School, and was then a resident Fellow
of Trinity College, Cambridge; his translation of
Sophocles is still well known. He dedicates his version of
Phalaris to John, Earl of Orrery, alluding to the esteem
in which the Greek author had been held by the late
Lord Orrery (Charles Boyle). He then refers to 'the
celebrated dispute' between Boyle and Bentley about
these Letters. 'Doctor Bentley,' he allows, 'was always
look'd on as a man of wit and parts.' On the other hand,
Francklin vindicates Boyle against 'the foolish opinion'
that he had been helped by 'some men of distinguished
merit' in his book against Bentley. Had this been so,
those men would have been eager to claim their share in

the reputation acquired by it. As they have not done so, there can be no reason why Boyle's 'claim to the deserved applause it has met with should ever for the future be call'd in question.' 'I have not enter'd into any of the points of the controversy,' Francklin proceeds, 'as it would be a disagreeable as well as unnecessary task, but shall only observe that, tho' *several very specious arguments are brought by Doctor Bentley, the strongest of them do only affect particular epistles ; which as Mr Boyle observes, do not hurt the whole body ;* for in a collection of pieces that have no dependence on each other, as epistles, epigrams, fables, the first number may be encreased by the wantonness and vanity of imitators in aftertimes, and *yet the book be authentic in the main, and an original still.*'

Francklin was not outraging the sense of a learned community by writing thus. In the very next year (1750) he was elected to the Regius Professorship of Greek. Nothing could show more conclusively the average state of literary opinion on the controversy half-a-century after it took place. But there is evidence which carries us fifty years lower still. In 1804 Cumberland, Bentley's grandson, was writing his *Memoirs.* 'I got together' (he says) 'all the tracts relative to the controversy between Boyle and Bentley, omitting none even of the authorities and passages they referred to, and having done this, I compressed the reasonings on both sides into a kind of statement and report upon the question in dispute; and if, in the result, my judgment went with him to whom my inclination lent, *no learned critic in the present age* will condemn me for the decision.' Such was the apologetic tone which Bentley's grandson still thought due to the world, even after Tyrwhitt had

written of the 'thunderbolt,' and Porson of the 'immortal
Dissertation'! The theory that Bentley had an immediate triumph does not represent the general impression
of his own age, but reflects the later belief of critical
scholars, who felt the crushing power of Bentley's reply,
and imagined that every one must have felt it when it
first appeared. The tamer account of the matter, besides
being the truer, is also far more really interesting. It
shows how long the clearest truth may have to wait.

Bentley's Dissertation was translated into Latin by
the Dutch scholar, John Daniel Lennep, who edited the
Letters of Phalaris. After Lennep's death, the translation and the edition were published together by
Valckenaer (1777). The Dissertation was subsequently
rendered into German, with notes, by Ribbeck ; and only
seven years ago (1874) the English text of the Dissertation (both in its first and in its second form) was reissued in Germany, with Introduction and notes, by Dr
Wilhelm Wagner. It has thus been the destiny of
Bentley's work, truly a work of genius, to become in
the best sense monumental. In a literature of which
continual supersession is the law, it has owed this permanent place to its triple character as a storehouse of
erudition, an example of method, and a masterpiece
of controversy. Isaac Disraeli justly said of it that 'it
heaves with the workings of a master spirit.' Bentley's
learning everywhere bears the stamp of an original mind;
and, even where it can be corrected by modern lights, has
the lasting interest of showing the process by which an
intellect of rare acuteness reached approximately true
conclusions. As a consecutive argument it represents the
first sustained application of strict reasoning to questions
of ancient literature—a domain in which his adversaries,

echoing the sentiment of their day, declared that 'all is
but a lucky guess.' As a controversial reply, it is little
less than marvellous, if we remember that his very
clever assailants had been unscrupulous in their choice of
weapons,—freely using every sort of insinuation, however
irrelevant or gross, which could tell,—and that Bentley
repulsed them at every point, without once violating the
usages of legitimate warfare. While he demolishes, one
by one, the whole series of their relevant remarks, he
steadily preserves his own dignity by simply turning
back upon them the dishonour of their own calumnies
and the ridicule of their own impertinence. With a
dexterity akin to that of a consummate debater, he wields
the power of retort in such a manner that he appears
to be hardly more than the amused spectator of a logical
recoil.

Shortly before Swift described Boyle as Achilles,
poor Achilles was writing from Ireland, in some per-
turbation of spirit, to those gods who were hard at work
on his armour, and confiding his hopes 'that it would do
no harm.' It did not do much. This was the first
controversy in English letters that had made anything
like a public stir, and it is pleasant to think that
Achilles and his antagonist appear to have been good
friends afterwards : if any ill-will lingered, it was rather
in the bosoms of the Myrmidons. Dr William King,
who had helped to make the mischief, never forgave
Bentley for his allusions to 'Humty-dumty,' and satirised
him in ten 'Dialogues of the Dead' (on Lucian's model)—
a title which suits their dulness. Bentley is Bentivoglio,
a critic who knows that the first weather-cock was set up
by the Argonauts and that cushions were invented by
Sardanapalus. Salter mentions a tradition, current in

1777, that Boyle, after he became Lord Orrery, visited
Bentley at Trinity College, Cambridge. There is contemporary evidence, not, indeed, for such personal intercourse, but for the existence of mutual esteem. In 1721
a weekly paper, 'The Spy,' attacked Bentley in an
article mainly patched up out of thefts from Boyle's
book on Phalaris, and a reply appeared, called 'The
Apothecary's Defence of Dr Bentley, in answer to the
Spy.' 'Let me now tell it the Spy as a secret,' says the
Apothecary, 'that Dr Bentley has the greatest deference
for his noble antagonist (Boyle), both as a person of eminent parts and quality; and I dare say his noble antagonist thinks of Dr Bentley as of a person as great in
critical learning as England has boasted of for many a
century.' We remember Bentley's description of Boyle
as 'a young gentleman of great hopes,' and gladly believe that the Apothecary was as well-informed as his
tone would imply. Atterbury was in later life on excellent terms with Bentley.

It is long enough now since 'the sprinkling of a
little dust' allayed the last throb of angry passion that
had been roused by the Battle of the Books: but we
look back across the years, and see more than the
persons of the quarrel; it was the beginning of a new
epoch in criticism; and it is marked by a work which,
to this hour, is classical in a twofold sense, in relation
to the literature of England and to the philology of
Europe.

CHAPTER VI.

Towards the end of 1699, about eight months after the publication of Bentley's Dissertation on Phalaris, the Mastership of Trinity College, Cambridge, became vacant by the removal of Dr Mountague to the Deanery of Durham. The nomination of a successor rested with six Commissioners, to whom King William had entrusted the duty of advising in the ecclesiastical and academic patronage of the Crown. They were Archbishops Tenison and Sharp, with Bishops Lloyd, Burnet, Patrick and Moore,—the last-named in place of Stillingfleet, who had died in April, 1699. On their unanimous recommendation, the post was given to Bentley. He continued to hold the office of King's Librarian; but his home thenceforth was at Cambridge.

No places in England have suffered so little as Oxford and Cambridge from the causes which tend to merge local colour in a monochrome. The academic world which Bentley entered is still, after a hundred and eighty years, comparatively near to us, both in form and in spirit. The visitor in 1700, whom the coach conveyed in twelve hours from the 'Bull' in Bishopsgate

Street to the 'Rose' in the Marketplace of Cambridge,
found a scene of which the essential features were the
same as they are to-day. The most distinctive among
the older buildings of the University had long been such
as we now see them; already for nearly two centuries
the chapel of King's College had been standing in the
completeness of its majestic beauty; the charm of the
past could already be felt in the quadrangles and cloisters
of many an ancient house, in pleasant shades and smooth
lawns by the quiet river, in gardens with margins of
bright flowers bordering time-stained walls, over which
the sound of bells from old towers came like an echo of
the middle age, in all the haunts which tradition linked
with domestic memories of cherished names. It was
only the environment of the University that was decidedly unlike the present. In the narrow streets of the
little town, where feeble oil-lamps flickered at night, the
projecting upper stories of the houses on either side
approached each other so nearly overhead as partly to
supply the place of umbrellas. The few shops that existed were chiefly open booths, with the goods displayed
on a board which also served as a shutter to close the
front. That great wilderness of peat-moss which once
stretched from Cambridge to the Wash had not yet been
drained with the thoroughness which has since reclaimed
two thousand square miles of the best corn-land in England; tracts of fen still touched the outskirts of the
town; snipe and marsh-fowl were plentiful in the present suburbs. To the south and south-east the country
was unenclosed, as it remained, in great measure, down
to the beginning of this century. A horseman might
ride for miles without seeing a fence.

The broadest difference between the University life

of Bentley's time and of our own might perhaps be
roughly described by saying that, for the older men, it
had more resemblance, both in its rigours and in its
laxities, to the life of a monastery, and, for the younger
men, to the life of a school. The College day began
with morning chapel, usually at six. Breakfast was not
a regular meal, but, from about 1700, it was often taken
at a coffee-house where the London newspapers could be
read. Morning lectures began at seven or eight in the
College hall. Tables were set apart for different subjects.
At 'the logick table' one lecturer is expounding Duncan's
treatise, while another, at 'the ethick table,' is interpreting Puffendorf on the Duty of a Man and a Citizen;
classics and mathematics engage other groups. The
usual College dinner-hour, which had long been 11 A.M.,
had advanced before 1720 to noon. The afternoon disputations in the Schools often drew large audiences to
hear 'respondent' and 'opponent' discuss such themes
as 'Natural Philosophy does not tend to atheism,' or
'Matter cannot think.' Evening chapel was usually at
five; a slight supper was provided in hall at seven or
eight; and at eight in winter, or nine in summer, the
College gates were locked. All students lodged within
College walls. Some tutors held evening lectures in
their rooms. Discipline was stern. The birch-rod which
was still hung up at the butteries typified a power in the
College dean similar to that which the fasces announced
in the Roman Consul; and far on in the seventeenth
century it was sometimes found to be more than an
austere symbol, when a youth showed himself, as
Anthony Wood has it, 'too forward, pragmatic, and
conceited.' Boating, in the athletic sense, was hardly
known till about 1820, and the first record of cricket in

its present form is said to be the match of Kent against England in 1746 ; but the undergraduates of Bentley's day played tennis, racquets, and bowls ; they rang peals on church-bells ; they gave concerts ; nay we hear that the votaries 'of Handel and Corelli' (the Italian violinist) were not less earnest than those of Newton and Locke. In Bentley's Cambridge the sense of a corporate life was strengthened by continuous residence. Many Fellows of Colleges, and some undergraduates, never left the University from one year's end to another. An excursion to the Bath or to Epsom Wells was the equivalent of a modern vacation-tour. No reading-party had yet penetrated to the Lakes or the Highlands. No summer fêtes yet brought an influx of guests ; the nearest approach to anything of the kind was the annual Sturbridge Fair in September, held in fields near the Cam, just outside the town. The seclusion of the University world is curiously illustrated by the humorous speeches which old custom allowed on certain public occasions. The sallies of the academic satirist were to the Cambridge of that period very much what the Old Comedy was for the Athens of Aristophanes. The citizens of a compact commonwealth could be sufficiently entertained by lively criticism of domestic affairs, or by pointed allusions to the conduct of familiar persons.

In relation to the studies of Cambridge the moment of Bentley's arrival was singularly opportune. The theories of Descartes had just been exploded by that Newtonian philosophy which Bentley's Boyle Lectures had first popularised ; in alliance with Newton's principles, a mathematical school was growing ; and other sciences also were beginning to flourish. Between 1702 and 1727 the University was provided with chairs of

Astronomy, Anatomy, Geology, and Botany; while the
academic study of Medicine was also placed on a better
footing.   George I. founded the chair of Modern History
in 1724.   For classical learning the latter part of the
seventeenth century had been a somewhat sterile period.
There was thus a twofold function for a man of comprehensive vigour, holding an eminent station in the
University,—to foster the new learning, and to reanimate
the old.   Bentley proved himself equal to both tasks.

On February 1, 1700, the Fellows of Trinity College
met in the chapel, for the purpose of admitting their
new Master.   Bentley took the Latin oath, promising
(among other undertakings) that he would 'observe in
all things the Statutes of the College, and interpret them
truly, sincerely, and according to their grammatical
sense;' that he would 'rule and protect all and singular
Fellows and Scholars, Pensioners, Sizars, Subsizars, and
the other members of the College, according to the same
Statutes and Laws, without respect of birth, condition,
or person, without favour or ill-will;' that, in the event
of his resigning or being deposed, he would restore all
that was due to the College 'without controversy or
tergiversation.'   He was then installed in the Master's
seat, and his reign began.

Bentley had just completed his thirty-eighth year.
He had a genius for scholarship, which was already
recognised.   He had also that which does not always
accompany it, a large enthusiasm for the advancement
of learning.   His powers of work were extraordinary,
and his physical strength was equal to almost any
demand which even he could make upon it.   Seldom
has a man of equal gifts been placed at so early an age
in a station which offered such opportunities.

Henry VIII. founded Trinity College only a few
weeks before his death. Two establishments, each more
than two centuries old, then stood on the site of the
present Great Court. One of these was Michael-house,
founded in 1324 by Hervey de Stanton, Chancellor to
Edward II. The other, King's Hall, was founded in
1337 by Edward III, who assigned it to the King's
Scholars, thirty or forty students, maintained at Cambridge by a royal bounty, first granted by Edward II.
in 1316. Thus, while Michael-house was the older
College, King's Hall represented the older foundation.
When Henry VIII. united them, the new name, 'Trinity
College,' was probably taken from Michael-house, which,
among other titles, had been dedicated to the Holy and
Undivided Trinity. The Reformation had been a crisis
in the history of the English Universities. In 1546 their
fortunes were almost at the lowest ebb. That fact adds
significance to the terms in which Henry's charter traces
the noble plan of Trinity College. The new house is
to be a 'college of literature, the sciences, philosophy, good
arts, and sacred Theology.' It is founded 'to the glory
and honour of Almighty God and the Holy and Undivided
Trinity; for the amplification and establishment of the
Christian faith; the extirpation of heresy and false
opinion; the increase and continuance of Divine Learning
and all kinds of good letters; the knowledge of the
tongues; the education of youth in piety, virtue,
learning and science; the relief of the poor, destitute
and afflicted; the prosperity of the Church of Christ;
and the common good of his kingdom and subjects.'

The King had died before this conception could be
embodied in legislative enactment. Statutes were made
for Trinity College in the reign of Edward VI., and
again in the reign of Mary. Manuscript copies of

these are preserved in the Muniment-room of the College; but the first printed code of Statutes was that given in the second year of Elizabeth. These governed Trinity College until a revision produced the 'Victorian' Statutes of 1844. Two features of the Elizabethan Statutes deserve notice. All the sixty Fellowships are left open, without appropriation to counties,—while at every other Cambridge College, except King's, territorial restrictions existed till this century. And, besides the College Lecturers, maintenance is assigned to three University Readers. These are the Regius Professors of Divinity, Hebrew and Greek, who are still on Henry VIII.'s foundation. Thus, from its origin, Trinity College was specially associated with two ideas:—free competition of merit; and provision, not only for collegiate tuition, but also for properly academic teaching.

During the first century of its life—from the reign of Edward VI. to the Civil Wars—the prosperity of Trinity College was brilliant and unbroken. The early days of the Great Rebellion were more disastrous for Cambridge than for Oxford; yet at Cambridge, as at Oxford, the period of the Commonwealth was one in which learning throve. Trinity College was 'purged' of its royalist members in 1645. Dr Thomas Hill then became Master. He proved an excellent administrator. Isaac Barrow, who was an undergraduate of the College, had written an exercise on 'the Gunpowder Treason,' in which his Cavalier sympathies were frankly avowed. Some of the Fellows were so much incensed that they moved for his expulsion, when Hill silenced them with the words, 'Barrow is a better man than any of us.' The last Master of Trinity before the Restoration was Dr John Wilkins, brother-in-law of Oliver Cromwell, and formerly Warden of Wadham College, Oxford; who was 'always

zealous to promote worthy men and generous designs.'
He was shrewdly suspected of being a royalist, and
Cromwell had been wont to greet his visits thus:—'What,
brother Wilkins, I suppose you are come to ask something or other in favour of the Malignants?' But his
influence is said to have decided the Protector against
confiscating the revenues of Oxford and Cambridge to
pay his army*.

In the space of forty years between the Restoration
and Bentley's arrival, Trinity College had suffered some
decline; not through any default of eminent abilities or
worthy characters, but partly from general influences
of the time, partly from the occasional want of a sufficiently firm rule.   Dr. John Pearson,—the author of
the treatise on the Creed,—was Master of Trinity from
1662 to 1673.   A contemporary—whose words plainly
show the contrast with Bentley which was in his mind—
said that Pearson was 'a man the least apt to encroach
upon anything that belonged to the Fellows, but treated
them all with abundance of civility and condescension.'
'The Fellows, he has heard, ask'd him whether he wanted
anything in his lodge,—table-linen, or the like;' "No,"
saith the good man, "I think not; this I have will serve
yet;" and though pressed by his wife to have new,
especially as it was offered him, he would refuse it while
the old was fit for use.   He was very well contented
with what the College allowed him.'

* See a letter, preserved in the Muniment-room of Trinity
College, Cambridge, and published by Mr W. Aldis Wright in *Notes
and Queries*, Aug. 13, 1881.   I may remark that Dr. Creyghton,
whose recollections in old age the letter reports, errs in one detail.
It must have been as Warden of Wadham, not as Master of
Trinity, that Wilkins interceded against the confiscation.   Oliver
Cromwell died Sept. 3, 1658.   It was early in 1659 that Richard
Cromwell appointed Wilkins to Trinity College.

Pearson was succeeded in the mastership by Isaac Barrow, who held it for only four years—from 1673 to his death in 1677. Both as a mathematician and as a theologian he stood in the foremost rank. In 1660 he was elected 'without a competitor' to the professorship of Greek. Thus a singular triad of distinctions is united in his person; as Lucasian professor of Mathematics, he was the predecessor of Newton; at Trinity College, of Bentley; and, in his other chair, of Porson. In early boyhood he was chiefly remarkable for his pugnacity, and for his aversion to books. When he was at Charterhouse, 'his greatest recreation was in such sports as brought on fighting among the boys; in his after-time a very great courage remained...yet he had perfectly subdued all inclination to quarrelling; but a negligence of his cloaths did always continue with him.' As Master of Trinity, 'besides the particular assistance he gave to many in their studies, he concerned himself in everything that was for the interest of his College.'

The next two Masters were men of a different type. John North was the fifth son of Dudley, Lord North, and younger brother of Francis North, first Baron Guilford, Lord Keeper in the reigns of Charles II. and James II. He had been a Fellow of Jesus College, and in 1677 he was appointed Master of Trinity. John North was a man of cultivated tastes and considerable accomplishments, of a gentle, very sensitive disposition, and of a highly nervous temperament. Even after he was a Fellow of his College, he once mistook a moonlit towel for 'an enorm spectre;' and his brother remembers how, at a still later period, 'one Mr Wagstaff, a little gentleman, had an express audience, at a very good dinner, on the subject of spectres, and much was said *pro* and *con.*' On one occasion he travelled into Wales, 'to visit and be possessed of his sinecure of Llandinon.' 'The parishioners came about him and hugged him, calling him their pastor, and telling him they were his sheep;' when 'he got him back to his College as fast as he could.' In the Mastership of Trinity North showed no weakness. Certain abuses had begun to infect the election to Fellowships, and he made a vigorous effort to remedy them. He was no less firm in his endeavours to revive discipline, which had been somewhat relaxed since the Restoration. One day he was in the act of admonishing two students, when he fell down in a fit. The two young men were 'very helpful' in carrying him to the Lodge. Paralysis of one side ensued. He lived for upwards of three years, but could thenceforth take little part in College affairs; and died, six years after he had become Master, in 1683.

Dr John Mountague, North's successor, was the fourth son of Edward, first Earl of Sandwich. The little that is known of Mountague exhibits him as an amiable person of courtly manners, who passed decently along the path of rapid preferment which then awaited a young divine with powerful connections. Having first been Master of Sherburn Hospital at Durham, he was appointed, in 1683, to the Mastership of Trinity. His easy temper and kindly disposition made him popular with the Fellows,—all the more so, perhaps, if his conscience was less exacting than that of the highly-strung, anxious North. In 1699 he returned, as Dean of Durham, to the scene of his earlier duties, and lived to see the fortunes of the College under Bentley. He died in London, in 1728. There was a double disadvantage for Bentley in coming after such a man; the personal contrast was marked; and those tendencies which North strove to repress had not suffered, under Mountague,

from any interference which exceeded the limits of good
breeding.

In the fore-front of the difficulties which met Bentley
Dr Monk puts the fact that he 'had no previous con-
nection with the College which he was sent to govern; he
was himself educated in another and a rival society.'
Now, without questioning that there were murmurs on
this score, I think that we shall overrate the influence
of such a consideration if we fail to observe what the
precedents had been up to that date. Bentley was the
twentieth Master since 1546. Of his nineteen predecessors, only five had been educated at Trinity College. To
take the four immediately preceding cases, Barrow and
Mountague had been of Trinity, but Pearson had been
of King's, and North of Jesus. Since Bentley's time
every Master has been of Trinity. But it cannot be
said that any established usage then existed of which
Bentley's appointment was a breach. And young though
he was for such a post,—thirty-eight,—he was not young
beyond recent example. Pearson, when appointed, had
been forty; Barrow, forty-three; North, thirty-three; and
Mountague, only twenty-eight. Thus the choice was not
decidedly exceptional in either of the two points which
might make it appear so now. But the task which, at
that moment, awaited a Master of Trinity was one which
demanded a rare union of qualities. How would Bentley
succeed? A few readers of the Dissertation on Phalaris,
that mock despot of Agrigentum, might tremble a little,
perhaps, at the thought that the scholarly author appeared
to have a robust sense of what a real tyrant should be,
and a cordial contempt for all shams in the part. It
was natural, however, to look with hope to his mental
grasp and vigour, his energy, his penetration, his genuine
love of learning.

CHAPTER VII.

WHEN Bentley entered on his new office, he was in one of those positions where a great deal may depend on the impression made at starting. He did not begin very happily. One of his first acts was to demand part of a College dividend due by usage to his predecessor, Dr Mountague, who closed the discussion by waiving his claim. Then the Master's Lodge required repairs, and the Seniority (the eight Senior Fellows) had voted a sum for that purpose, but the works were executed in a manner which ultimately cost about four times the amount. It is easy to imagine the comments and comparisons to which such things would give rise in a society not, perhaps, too favourably prepossessed towards their new chief. But Bentley's first year at Trinity is marked by at least one event altogether fortunate,—his marriage. At Bishop Stillingfleet's house he had·met Miss Joanna Bernard, daughter of Sir John Bernard, of Brampton, Huntingdonshire. 'Being now raised to a station of dignity and consequence, he succeeded in obtaining the object of his affections,' says Dr Monk—who refuses to believe a story that the engagement was nearly broken off owing to a doubt expressed by Bentley with regard to the authority of the Book of Daniel. Whiston has told us what this alleged doubt was. Nebuchadnezzar's golden image is described as sixty cubits high and six cubits broad ; now, said Bentley, this is out of all proportion ; it ought to have been ten cubits broad at least ; 'Which made the good lady weep.' The lovers' difference was possibly arranged on the basis suggested by Whiston, —that the sixty cubits included the pedestal. Some letters which passed between Dr Bentley and Miss Bernard, before their marriage, are still extant, and have been printed by Dr Luard at the end of Rud's *Diary*. In the Library of Trinity College is preserved a small printed and interleaved 'Ephemeris' for the year 1701. The blank page opposite the month of January has the following entries in Bentley's hand :—

Jan. 4. I maried Mrs Johanna Bernard, daughter of Sr John Bernard, Baronet. Dr Richardson, Fellow of Eaton College and Master of Peterhouse, maried us at Windsor in ye College Chapel.

6. I brought my wife to St James's. [*i.e.* to his Lodgings, as King's Librarian, in the Palace.]

27. I am 39 years old, complete.

28. I returnd to ye College.

It was a thoroughly happy marriage, through forty years of union. What years they were, too, outside of the home in which Mrs Bentley's gentle presence dwelt ! In days when evil tongues were busy, no word is said of her but in praise ; and perhaps, if all were known, few women ever went through more in trying, like Mrs Thrale, to be civil for two.

Bentley was Vice-Chancellor of Cambridge at the time of his marriage. His year of office brought him into collision with the gaieties of that great East England carnival, Sturbridge Fair. Its entertainments were under the joint control of the University and the Town, but, without licence from the Vice-Chancellor, some actors had been announced to play in September, 1701. Bentley interposed his veto, and provided for discipline by investing sixty-two Masters of Arts with the powers of Proctors. One of his last acts as Vice-Chancellor was to draw up an address which the University presented to King William, expressing 'detestation of the indignity' which Louis XIV. had just offered to the English Crown by recognising the claims of the Pretender.

The term of his University magistracy having expired, Bentley was able to bestow undivided attention on Trinity College. An important reform was among his earliest measures. Fellowships and Scholarships were at that time awarded by a merely oral examination. Written papers were now introduced; the competition for Scholarships became annual instead of biennial, and freshmen were admitted to it. The permanent value of this change is not affected by the estimate which may be formed of Bentley's personal conduct in College elections. There are instances in which it was represented as arbitrary and unfair. But we must remember that his behaviour was closely watched by numerous enemies, who eagerly pressed every point which could be plausibly urged against him. The few detailed accounts which we have of the elections give the impression that, in those cases at least, the merits of candidates were fairly considered. Thus John Byrom says (1709):—'We were examined by the Master, Vice Master, and Dr Smith, one of the Seniors. On Wednesday we made theme for Dr Bentley, and on Thursday the Master and Seniors met in the Chapel for the election [to scholarships.] Dr Smith

H 2

had the gout and was not there. They stayed consulting
about an hour and a half, and then the Master wrote the
names of the elect and gave them to the Chapel Clerk.'
Whether he was or was not always blameless on such
occasions, Bentley deserves to be remembered as the
Master who instituted a better machinery for testing
merit, and provided better guarantees for its recognition.

To do him justice, no man could have been more
earnest than Bentley was in desiring to maintain the
prestige of Trinity College, or more fully sensible of the
rank due to it in science and letters. It was through
Bentley's influence that the newly-founded Plumian
Professorship of Astronomy was conferred on Roger
Cotes—then only a Bachelor of Arts—who was provided
with an observatory in the rooms over the Great Gate of
Trinity College (1706). Ten years later, when this man
of wonderful promise died at the age of thirty-four,
Newton said—'Had Cotes lived, we should have known
something.' The appointment of Cotes may be regarded
as marking the formal establishment of a Newtonian
school in Cambridge; and it was of happy omen that it
should have been first lodged within the walls which had
sheltered the labours of the founder. Three English
Sovereigns visited the College in the course of Bentley's
Mastership, but the most interesting fact connected with
any of these occasions is the public recognition of
Newton's scientific eminence in 1705, when he received
knighthood from Queen Anne at Trinity Lodge. Then
it was Bentley who fitted up a chemical laboratory in
Trinity College for Vigani, a native of Verona, who,
after lecturing in Cambridge for some years, was
appointed Professor of Chemistry in 1702. It was
Bentley who made Trinity College the home of the

eminent oriental scholar Sike, of Bremen, whom he
helped to obtain the Regius Chair of Hebrew in 1703.
Briefly, wherever real science needed protection or
encouragement, there, in Bentley's view, was the opportunity of Trinity College; it was to be indeed a house of
the sciences and 'of all kinds of good letters'; it was to
be not only a great College, but, in its own measure, a
true University.

This noble conception represents the good side of
Bentley's Mastership; he did something towards making
it a reality; he did more still towards creating, or re-
animating, a tradition that this is what Trinity College
was meant to be, and that nothing lower than this is the
character at which it should aim. Nor is it without
significance that Nevile's care for the external embellish-
ment of the College was resumed by Bentley. The
Chapel, begun in 1557 and finished in Elizabeth's reign,
was through Bentley's efforts entirely refitted, and
furnished with a fine organ by Bernard Smith. This
work was completed in 1727. The grounds beyond the
river, acquired by Nevile, were first laid out by Bentley;
and the noble avenue of limes, planted in 1674 on the
west side of the Cam, was continued in 1717 from the
bridge to the College.

But unfortunately it was his resolve to be absolute,
and he proclaimed it in a manner which was altogether
his own. The College Bursar (a Fellow) having protested
against the lavish outlay on the repairs of the Master's
Lodge, Bentley said that he would 'send him into the
country to feed his turkeys.' When the Fellows opposed
him in the same matter, he alluded to his power, under
the Statutes, of forbidding them to leave the College,
and cried, 'Have you forgotten my rusty sword?' The

Fellow who held the office of Junior Bursar had demurred to paying for a hen-house which had been put
in the Master's yard; Bentley, doubtless in allusion
to Lafontaine's fable of 'the Old Lion,' replied, 'I will
not be kicked by an *ass*,'—and presently strained his
prerogative by stopping the Junior Bursar's commons.
Remonstrances being made, he grimly rejoined, "'Tis all
but *lusus jocusque* (mere child's-play); I am not warm
yet.' Criticising a financial arrangement which was
perfectly legitimate, but of which he disapproved, he
accused the Seniors of 'robbing the Library,' and 'putting
the money in their own pockets.' He harassed the
society by a number of petty regulations, in which we
may give him credit for having aimed at a tonic effect,
but which were so timed and executed as to be highly
vexatious. Thus, in order to force the Fellows to take the
higher degrees, he procured the decision, after a struggle,
that any Bachelor or Doctor of Divinity should have a
right to College rooms or a College living before a Master
of Arts, even though the latter was senior on the list of
Fellows. As a measure of retrenchment, he abolished
the entertainment of guests by the College at the great
festivals. Taking the dead letter of the statutes in its
rigour, he decreed that the College Lecturers should be
fined if they omitted to perform certain daily exercises
in the hall, which were no longer needful or valuable; he
also enforced, in regard to the thirty junior Fellows, petty
fines for absence from chapel (which were continued
to recent times). On several occasions he took into his
own hands a jurisdiction which belonged to him only
jointly with the eight Seniors. Thus, in one instance, he
expelled two Fellows of the College by his sole fiat.

If Bentley is to be credited with the excellence of

the intentions which declared themselves in such a form, recognition is certainly due to the forbearance shown by the Fellows of Trinity. Bentley afterwards sought to represent them as worthless men who resented his endeavours to reform them. It cannot be too distinctly said that this was totally unjust. The Fellows, as a body, were liable to no such charges as Bentley in his anger brought against them; not a few of them were eminent in the University; and if there were any whose lives would not bear scrutiny, they were at most two or three, usually non-resident, and always without influence. It may safely be said that no large society of that time, in either University, would have sustained an inspection with more satisfactory results. The average College Fellow of that period was a moderately accomplished clergyman, whose desire was to repose in decent comfort on a small freehold. Bentley swooped on a large house of such persons,—not ideal students, yet, on the whole, decidedly favourable specimens of their kind; he made their lives a burden to them, and then denounced them as the refuse of humanity when they dared to lift their heads against his insolent assumption of absolute power. They bore it as long as flesh and blood could. For nearly eight years they endured. At last, in December, 1709, things came to a crisis,—almost by an accident.

Bentley had brought forward a proposal for re-distributing the divisible income of the College according to a scheme of his own, one feature of which was that the Master should receive a dividend considerably in excess of his legitimate claims. Even Bentley's authority failed to obtain the acquiescence of the Seniors in this novel interpretation of the maxim, *divide et impera.*

They declined to sanction the scheme. While the discussion was pending, Edmund Miller, a lay Fellow, came up to spend the Christmas vacation at Trinity. As an able barrister, who understood College business, he was just such an ally as the Fellows needed. He found them, he says, 'looking like so many prisoners, which were uncertain whether to expect military execution, or the favour of decimation.' At a meeting of the Master and Seniors, it was agreed to hear Miller, as a representative of the junior Fellows, on the dividend question. Miller denounced the plan to Bentley's face, who replied by threatening to deprive him of his Fellowship. A few days later, an open rupture took place between the Seniors and Bentley, who left the room exclaiming, 'Henceforward, farewell peace to Trinity College.' Miller now drew up a declaration, which was signed by twenty-four resident Fellows, including the Seniors. It expressed a desire that Bentley's conduct should be represented 'to those who are the proper judges thereof, and in such manner as counsel shall advise.' Bentley, against the unanimous vote of the Seniors, and on a technical quibble of his own, now declared Miller's Fellowship void. Miller appealed to the Vice-Master, who, supported by all the Seniors, replaced him on the list. The Master again struck out his name. Miller now left for London. Bentley soon followed. Both sides were resolved on war.

Who were 'the proper judges' of Bentley's conduct? The 46th chapter of Edward VI.'s Statutes for Trinity College recognised the Bishop of Ely as General Visitor. The Elizabethan Statutes omit this, but in their 40th chapter, which provides for the removal of the Master in case of necessity, incidentally speak of the Bishop as

Visitor. Bentley, six years before (1703), had himself appealed to the Bishop of Ely on a point touching the Master's prerogative. No other precedent existed. Acting on this, the Fellows, in February, 1710, laid their 'humble petition and complaint' before the Bishop of Ely. They brought, in general terms, a charge of malversation against Bentley, and promised to submit 'the several particulars' within a convenient time. Bentley now published a 'Letter to the Bishop of Ely,' in which he made a most gross attack on the collective character of the Fellows,—describing their Petition as 'the last struggle and effort of vice and idleness against vertue, learning, and good discipline.' In July, the Fellows presented 'the several particulars' to the Bishop, in the form of an accusation comprising fifty-four counts. The Statute prescribed that an accused Master should be 'examined' before the Visitor. Hence each of the counts is interrogative. For example :—

'Why have you for many Years last past, wasted the College Bread, Ale, Beer, Coals, Wood, Turfe, Sedge, Charcoal, Linnen, Pewter, Corn, Flower, Brawn, and Bran ? &c.'

'When by false and base Practices, as by threatning to bring Letters from Court, Visitations, and the like ; and at other times, by boasting of your great Interest and Acquaintance, and that you were the Genius of the Age, and what great things you would do for the College in general, and for every Member of it in particular, and promising that you would for the future live peaceably with them, and never make any farther Demands, you had prevailed with the Senior Fellows to allow you several hundred Pounds for your Lodge, more than they first intended or agreed for, to the great Dissatisfaction of the College, and the wonder of the whole University, and all that heard of it : Why did you the very next Year, about that time, merely for your own Vanity, require them to build you a new Stair-case in your Lodge? 𝕬𝖓𝖉 𝖜𝖍𝖊𝖓 they (considering how much you had extorted from them before, which you had never accounted for) did for good reason deny to do it; 𝖂𝖍𝖞 did you of your own Head pull down a good Stair-case in your Lodge, and give Orders and Directions for building a new one, and that too fine for common Use?'

'𝖂𝖍𝖞 did you use scurrilous Words and Language to several of the Fellows, particularly by calling Mr *Eden* an Ass, and Mr *Rashly* the College Dog, and by telling Mr *Cock* he would die in his Shoes?'

Dr Moore, the learned Bishop of Ely, was one of the six Commissioners who had nominated Bentley for the Mastership; he sympathised with his studies; and Bentley had been Archdeacon of the diocese since 1701. The judge, then, could hardly be suspected of any bias against the accused. He sent a copy of the accusation to Bentley, who ignored it for some months. In November the Bishop wrote again, requiring a reply by December 18. Bentley then petitioned the Queen, praying that the Bishop of Ely might be restrained from usurping the functions of Visitor. The Visitor of Trinity College, Bentley contended, was the Sovereign. Mr Secretary St John at once referred Bentley's contention to the Law Officers of the Crown, and meanwhile the Bishop was inhibited from proceeding. This was at the end of 1710.

Bentley's move was part of a calculation. In 1710 the Tories had come in under Harley and St John. Mrs Bentley was related to St John, and also to Mr Masham, whose wife had succeeded the Duchess of Marlborough in the Queen's favour. Bentley reckoned on commanding sufficient influence to override the Bishop's jurisdiction by a direct interposition of the Crown. He was disappointed. The Attorney General and the Solicitor General reported that, in their opinion, the Bishop of Ely

was Visitor of Trinity College in matters concerning the
Master; adding that Bentley could, if he pleased, try
the question in a court of law. This was not what
Bentley desired. He now wrote to the Prime Minister,
Harley, who had recently escaped assassination, and,
with the office of Lord High Treasurer, had been created
Earl of Oxford. Bentley's letter is dated July 12, 1711.
'I desire nothing more,' he writes, 'than that her Majesty
would send down commissioners to examine into all
matters upon the place,...and to punish where the faults
shall be found...I am easy under everything but loss of
time by detainment here in town, which hinders me
from putting my last hand to my edition of Horace, and
from doing myself the honour to inscribe it to your
Lordship's great name.' The Premier did his best. He
referred the report of the Attorney and Solicitor to the
Lord Keeper, Sir Simon Harcourt, and Queen's Counsel.
In January, 1712, they expressed their opinion that the
Sovereign is the General Visitor of Trinity College, but
that the Bishop of Ely is Special Visitor in the case of
charges brought against the Master. The Minister now
tried persuasion with the Fellows. Could they not con-
cur with the Master in referring their grievances to the
Crown? The Fellows declined. A year passed. Bentley
tried to starve out the College by refusing to issue a
dividend. In vain. The Ministry were threatened with
a revision, in the Queen's Bench, of their veto on the
Bishop. They did not like this prospect. On April 18,
1713, Bolingbroke, as Secretary of State, authorised the
Bishop of Ely to proceed.

Bentley's ingenuity was not yet exhausted. He proposed that the trial should be held forthwith at Cambridge,
where all the College books were ready to hand. Had

this been done, he must certainly have been acquitted,
since the prosecutors had not yet worked up their case.
Some of the Fellows unwarily consented. But the
Bishop appointed Ely House in London as the place of
trial, and the month of November, 1713, as the time.
Various causes of delay intervened. At last, in May,
1714, the trial came on in the great hall of Ely House.
Five counsel, including Miller, were employed for the
Fellows, and three for Bentley. Bishop Moore had two
eminent lawyers as his assessors,—Lord Cowper, an ex-
chancellor, and Dr Newton. Public feeling was at first
with Bentley, as a distinguished scholar and divine.
But the prosecutors had a strong case. An anecdote of
the trial is given by Bentley's grandson, Cumberland.
One day the Bishop intimated, from his place as judge,
that he condemned the Master's conduct. For once,
Bentley's iron nerve failed him. He fainted in court.

After lasting six weeks, the trial ended about the
middle of June. Both sides now awaited with intense
anxiety the judgment of the Bishop and his assessors.
The prosecutors were confident. But week after week
elapsed in silence. The Bishop had caught a chill during
the sittings. On July 31, he died. The next day,
August 1, 1714, London was thrilled by momentous news.
Queen Anne was no more. The British Crown had
passed to the House of Hanover. Ministers had fallen ;
new men were coming to power ; the political world
was wild with excitement ; and the griefs of Trinity
College would have to wait.

Bentley's escape had been narrow. After Bishop
Moore's death, the judgment which he had prepared, but
not pronounced, was found among his papers. ' By
this our definitive sentence, we remove Richard Bentley

from his office of Master of the College.' Dr Monk thinks that the Bishop had meant this merely to frighten Bentley into a compromise with the Fellows. Possibly : though in that case the Bishop would have had to reckon with the other side. But in any case Bentley must have accepted the Bishop's terms, and these must have been such as would have satisfied the prosecutors. If not ejected, therefore, he would still have been defeated. As it was, he got off scot-free.

The new Bishop of Ely, Dr Fleetwood, took a different line from his predecessor. The Crown lawyers had held that the Bishop was Special Visitor, but not General Visitor. Dr Fleetwood said that, if he interfered at all, it must be as General Visitor, to do justice on all alike. This scared some of the weaker Fellows into making peace with Bentley, who kindly consented to drop his dividend scheme. In one sense the new Bishop's course was greatly to Bentley's advantage, since it raised the preliminary question over again. Miller vainly tried to move Dr Fleetwood. Meanwhile Bentley was acting as autocrat of the College,—dealing with its property and its patronage as he pleased. His conduct led to a fresh effort for redress.

The lead on this occasion was taken by Dr Colbatch, now a Senior Fellow. From the beginning of the feuds, Colbatch had been a counsellor of moderation, disapproving much in the stronger measures advocated by Miller. He was an able and accomplished man, whose rigid maintenance of his own principles extorted respect even where it did not command sympathy. Colbatch's early manhood had been expended on performing the duties of private tutor in two families of distinction, and he had returned to College at forty, more convinced

than ever that it is a mistake to put trust in princes.
He was a dangerous enemy because he seemed incapable
of revenge; it was always on high grounds that he
desired the confusion of the wicked ; and he pursued that
object with the temperate implacability which belongs to
a disappointed man of the world. Since the Bishop of
Ely would not act unless as General Visitor, Colbatch
drew up a petition, which nineteen Fellows signed,
praying that it might be ascertained who was General
Visitor. This was encouraged by the Archbishop of
Canterbury, Dr Wake,—who described Bentley as 'the
greatest instance of human frailty that I know of, as
with such good parts and so much learning he can be
so insupportable.' The object of the petition was baulked
for the time by the delays of the Attorney General.
After three years the petition came before the Privy
Council in May, 1719.

Bentley was equal to the occasion. Serjeant Miller had
presented the petition, and could withdraw it. For five
years Bentley had been making active war on Miller, and
renewing the attempt to eject him from his Fellowship.
Now, towards the end of 1719, he made peace with him,
on singular terms. Miller was to withdraw the petition; to
resign his Fellowship, in consideration of certain payments;
and to receive the sum of £400 as costs on account of the
former prosecution before Bishop Moore. Miller agreed.
Bentley then proposed the compact to the Seniors. Five
of the eight would have nothing to say to it. By a
series of manœuvres, however, Bentley carried it at a
subsequent meeting. Serjeant Miller received £528 from
the College. Who shall describe the feelings of the
belligerent Fellows, when the Serjeant's strategy collapsed
in this miserable Sedan? It was he who had made them

go to war; it was he who had led them through the
mazes of the law; they had caught his clear accents,
learned his great language; and here was the end of it!
But this was not all. If the College is to pay costs on
one side, the Master argued, it must pay them on both.
Accordingly, Bentley himself received £500 for his own
costs in the trial. And, anxious to make hay in this
gleam of sunshine, he further prevailed on the Seniors
to grant a handsome sum for certain furniture of the
Master's Lodge. Bentley had no more to fear, at
present, from the opposition of an organised party. For
the next few years his encounters were single combats.

Such was the state of affairs in Trinity College.
Meanwhile Bentley's relations with the University had
come to an extraordinary pass. From the first days of
his Mastership, his reputation, his ability and energy had
made him influential in Cambridge, though he was not
generally popular. We saw that, before his appointment
to Trinity, he had taken a leading part in the reparation
of the University Press. He continued to show an active
interest in its management by serving on occasional
committees; no permanent Press Syndicate was consti-
tuted till 1737. Politics were keen at the University in
Bentley's time : a division in the academic Senate was
often a direct trial of strength between Whig and Tory.
When Bentley struck a blow in these University battles,
it was almost always with a view to some advantage in
his own College war. Two instances will illustrate this.
In June, 1712, when acting as Deputy Vice-Chancellor,
Bentley carried in the Senate an address to Queen Anne,
congratulating her on the progress of the peace negotiations at Utrecht. The address was meant as a manifesto
in support of the Tory Ministry, whom the Whigs had

just been attacking on this score in the Lords. At that
time, Harley, the Tory Premier, was the protector on
whom Bentley relied in his College troubles. The
irritation of the Whig party in the University may have
been one cause of a severe reflection passed on Bentley
soon afterwards. The Senate resolved that no Archdeacon of Ely should thenceforth be eligible as Vice-
Chancellor; a decree which, however, was rescinded two
years later. Then in 1716 Bentley sorely needed the
countenance of the Whig Government against the revived
hostilities in Trinity. By a surprise, he carried through
the Senate an address to George I., congratulating him on
the recent suppression of the Jacobite risings. A letter
of Bentley's describes the Cambridge Tories as being 'in
a desperate rage,'—not wholly, perhaps, without provo-
cation.

It was shortly before this,—in the early days of
the Jacobite rebellion, when visions of a Roman Catholic
reign were agitating the public imagination,—that
Bentley preached before the University, on the fifth of
November, 1715, his 'Sermon on Popery,'—from which
a passage on the tortures of the Inquisition has been
transferred by Sterne to the pages of Tristram Shandy,
and deeply moves Corporal Trim. Bentley had then
lately received the unusual honour of being publicly
thanked by the Senate for his reply to 'A Discourse of
Free-Thinking' by Anthony Collins. When the Regius
Professorship of Divinity—the most valuable in the
University—fell vacant in 1717, few persons, perhaps,
would have questioned Dr Bentley's claims on the
grounds of ability and learning. But the Statute had
declared that the Professor must not hold any other
office in the University or in Trinity College. Two

precedents were alleged to show that a Master of Trinity
might hold the Professorship, but they were not unex-
ceptionable. Of the seven electors, three certainly—
presumably five—were against the Master of Trinity's
pretensions. The favourite candidate was Dr Ashton,
Master of Jesus; and there are letters to him which
show the strong feeling in the University against his
rival. On the whole, most men would have despaired.
Not so Bentley. By raising a legal point, he contrived
to stave off the election for a few weeks; and then
seized a propitious moment. The Vice-Chancellor was
one of the seven electors. It was arranged that Mr Grigg,
who held that office, should leave Cambridge for a few
days, naming Bentley Deputy Vice-Chancellor. On the
day of election, the Master of Trinity was chosen Regius
Professor of Divinity by four out of seven votes, one
of the four being that of the Deputy Vice-Chancellor.
It was in this candidature that Dr Bentley delivered
an admired discourse on the three heavenly witnesses,
which denied the authenticity of that text. It is no
longer extant, but had been seen by Porson, who himself
wrote on the subject.

This was in May, 1717. Not long afterwards Bentley
had occasion to appear publicly in his new character of
Regius Professor. Early in October, George I. was
staying at Newmarket. On Friday, the 4th, his Majesty
consented to visit Cambridge on the following Sunday.
There was not much time for preparation, but it was
arranged to confer the degree of Doctor of Laws on
twenty-seven of the royal retinue, and that of Doctor of
Divinity on thirty-two members of the University.
On Sunday morning Mr Grigg, the Vice-Chancellor,
presented himself at Trinity Lodge, there to await the

arrival of the Chancellor, 'the proud Duke of Somerset.'
Bentley was unprepared for this honour; he was 'in his
morning gown,' busied with meditations of hospitality or
of eloquence; in fact, he remonstrated; but Mr Grigg
remained. At last the Chancellor came. Bentley was
affable, but a little *distrait*. 'While he entertained the
Duke in discourse,' (says one who was present,) 'there
stood the Earl of Thomond and Bishop of Norwich,
unregarded: and there they might have stood, if one of
the Beadles had not touched his sleeve a little; and then
he vouchsafed them a welcome also.' But worse was to
come. George I. attended service at King's College
Chapel. When it was over, the Vice-Chancellor proceeded to conduct his Majesty back to Trinity College.
But Mr Grigg was desirous that royal eyes should behold
his own College, Clare Hall, and therefore chose a route
which led to a closed gate of Trinity College. Here a
halt of some minutes took place in a muddy lane, before
word could reach the principal entrance, where Bentley
and an enthusiastic crowd were awaiting their Sovereign.

These little griefs, however, were nothing to the later
troubles which this day's proceedings begat for Bentley.
As it was thought that thirty-two new Doctors of
Divinity might be too much for the King, Sunday's
ceremonial had been limited to presenting a few of them
as samples. Bentley, as Regius Professor of Divinity,
had done his part admirably. But the next day, when
the rest of the doctors were to be 'created' at leisure,
Bentley flatly refused to proceed, unless each of them
paid him a fee of four guineas, in addition to the customary broad-piece. As the degrees were honorary, the
claim was sheer extortion. Some complied, others
resisted. Conyers Middleton, the biographer of Cicero,

was at this time a resident in Cambridge, though no
longer a Fellow of any College. He paid his four guineas,
got his D.D. degree, and then sued Bentley for the debt in
the Vice-Chancellor's Court, a tribunal of academic jurisdiction in such matters. After months of fruitless
diplomacy, the Vice-Chancellor reluctantly issued a
decree for Bentley's arrest at Middleton's suit. The writ
was served on Bentley at Trinity Lodge,—not, however,
before one of the Esquire Bedells had been treated with
indignity. Bail was given for Bentley's appearance
before the Court on October 3, 1718. He failed to appear.
The Court then declared that he was suspended from all
his degrees. A fortnight later, a Grace was offered to
the Senate, proposing that Bentley's degrees should be
not merely suspended but taken away. Bentley's friends
did their utmost. To the honour of the Fellows of
Trinity, only four of them voted against him. But the
Grace was carried by more than two to one. Nine
Heads of Colleges and twenty-three Doctors supported it.

When the Master of Trinity learned that he was no
longer Richard Bentley, D.D., M.A., or even B.A., but
simply Richard Bentley, he said, 'I have rubbed
through many a worse business than this.' He instantly
bestirred himself with his old vigour, petitioning the
Crown, appealing to powerful friends, and dealing some
hard knocks in the free fight of pamphlets which broke out
on the question. For nearly six years, however, he remained under the sentence of degradation. During that period
he brought actions of libel against his two principal adversaries, Colbatch, and Conyers Middleton. Colbatch
suffered a week's imprisonment and a fine. Middleton
was twice prosecuted; the first time, he had to apologise
to Bentley, and pay costs; the second time he was fined.

During the years 1720—1723 Bentley had altogether six law-suits in the Court of King's Bench, and gained all of them. The last and most important was against the University, for having taken away his degrees. That act had undoubtedly been illegal. The four judges all took Bentley's part. On February 7, 1724, the Court gave judgment. The University received peremptory direction to restore Bentley's degrees. That command was obeyed, but with a significant circumstance. On March 25, 1724, the Vice-Chancellor was to lay the first stone of the new buildings designed for King's College. In order that Bentley might not participate as a Doctor in the ceremonial, the Grace restoring his degrees was offered to the Senate on March 26.

Thus, after fifteen years of almost incessant strife, the Master of Trinity had prevailed over opposition both in the College and in the University. He was sixty-two. His fame as a scholar was unrivalled. As a controversialist he had proved himself a match, in different fields, for wits, heretics, and lawyers. At Cambridge, where he was now the virtual leader of the Whig party in the Senate, his influence had become pre-eminent. And as if to show that he had passed through all his troubles without stain, it was in this year, 1724, that the Duke of Newcastle wrote and offered him the Bishopric of Bristol,—then rather a poor one. Bentley declined it, frankly observing that the revenues of the see would scarcely enable him to attend Parliament. When he was asked what preferment he would accept,— 'Such,' he answered, 'as would not induce me to desire an exchange.'

The remainder of this combative life, it might have been thought, would now be peaceful. But the last

chapter is the most curious of all. It can be briefly
told. Dr Colbatch, the ablest of Bentley's adversaries
in Trinity College, had never resigned the purpose of
bringing the Master to justice. It had become the
object for which he lived : private wrongs had sunk into
his mind ; but he believed himself to be fulfilling a public
duty. In 1726 he vainly endeavoured to procure intervention by the Dean and Chapter of Westminster, on
the ground of certain grievances suffered by the Westminster scholars at Trinity College. In 1728 he was
more successful. Some Fellows of Trinity joined him in
a fresh attempt to obtain a visitation of the College by
the Bishop of Ely. There was, in fact, good reason for
it. Bentley's rule had become practically absolute, and
therefore unconstitutional. While Colbatch's new allies
were preparing their measures, death nearly saved them
the trouble. George II. had visited Cambridge, and
had been received in full state at Trinity College.
Bentley, who was subject to severe colds, had caught
a chill during the ceremonies of the reception, in the
course of which he had been called on to present no
fewer than fifty-eight Doctors of Divinity. He was
seized with fever. For some days his life was in most
imminent danger. But he rallied, and, after taking
the waters at Bath, recovered. Five Counsel having
expressed an opinion that the Bishop of Ely was General
Visitor of the College, Dr Greene, who now held that
see, cited Bentley to appear before him. Bentley did
so ; but presently obtained a rule from the Court of
King's Bench, staying the Bishop's proceedings on the
ground that the articles of accusation included matters
not cognizable by the Bishop. The question of the
Bishop's jurisdiction was next brought before the King's

Bench. The Court decided that the Bishop was in this cause Visitor, but again stayed his proceedings—this time on the ground of a technical informality. The prosecutors now appealed to the House of Lords. The House of Lords reversed the decision of the King's Bench, and empowered the Bishop to try Bentley on twenty of the sixty-four counts which had been preferred.

After the lapse of nearly twenty years, Bentley was once more arraigned at Ely House. This second trial began on June 13, 1733. On April 27, 1734, the Bishop gave judgment. Bentley was found guilty of dilapidating the College goods and violating the College Statutes. He was sentenced to be deprived of the Mastership.

At last the long chase was over and the prey had been run to earth. No shifts or doublings could save him now. It only remained to execute the sentence. The Bishop sent down to Cambridge three copies of his judgment. One was for Bentley. Another was to be posted on the gates of Trinity College. A third was to be placed in the hands of the Vice-Master.

The fortieth Statute of Elizabeth, on which the judgment rested, prescribes that the Master, if convicted by the Visitor, shall be deprived *by the agency of the Vice-Master*. It has been thought—and Monk adopts the view—that the word *Vice-Master* here is a mere clerical error for *Visitor*. The tenor of the Statute itself first led me to doubt this plausible theory. For it begins by saying that a peccant Master shall first be *admonished* by the Vice-Master and Seniors: *per Vice Magistrum* etc...*admoneatur*. If obdurate, he is then to be examined by the Visitor; and, if convicted, *per eundem Vice-Magistrum*

Officio Magistri privetur. This seems to mean :—'let
him be *deprived* by the same Vice-Master who had
first *admonished* him.' The Statute intended to provide
for the *execution* of the sentence by the College itself, without the scandal of any external intervention
beyond the purely *judicial* interposition of the Visitor.
I have since learned that the late Francis Martin,
formerly Vice-Master, discussed this point in a short
paper (Nov. 12, 1857), which Dr Luard's kindness has
enabled me to see. Dr Monk had seen a copy of the
statutes in which *Visitatorem* was written as a correction
over *Vice-Magistrum.* He believed this copy to be the
original one : and when in 1846 Martin showed him the
really authentic copy—with Elizabeth's signature and
the Great Seal—in the Muniment-room, he at once said,
'I never saw that book.' There the words stand clearly
Vice-Magr̄m, as in the statutes of Philip and Mary :
there is no correction, superscript or marginal : and the
vellum shows that there has been no erasure. The Vice-
Master, who takes the chief part in admitting the Master
(Stat. Cap. 2), is the natural minister of deprivation.
Bentley's Counsel advised the Vice-Master, Dr Hacket,
to refrain from acting until he had taken legal opinion.
Meanwhile Bentley continued to act as Master, to the
indignation of his adversaries, and the astonishment of the
world. An examination for College scholarships was going
on just then. On such occasions in former years Bentley
had often set the candidates to write on some theme
suggestive of his own position. Thus, at the height of his
monarchy, he gave them, from Virgil,—'*No one of this
number shall go away without a gift from me*': and once, at
a pinch in his wars, from Homer,—'*Despoil others, but keep
hands off Hector.*' This time he had a very apposite text for

the young composers, from Terence : '*This is your plea
now,—that I have been turned out : look you, there are ups
and downs in all things.*'   Dr Hacket, however, had no
mind to stand long in the breach ; and on May 17, 1734,
he resigned the Vice-Mastership.   He was succeeded by
Dr Richard Walker, a friend on whom Bentley could
rely.   During the next four years, every resource which
ingenuity could suggest was employed to force Dr
Walker into executing the sentence of deprivation on
Bentley.   A petition was presented by Colbatch's party
to the House of Lords, which the peers, after a debate,
permitted to be withdrawn.   Dr Walker now effected a
compromise between Bentley and some of the hostile
Fellows.   But Colbatch persevered.   Three different
motions were made in the Court of King's Bench ; first,
for a writ to compel Dr Walker to act ; next, for a writ
to compel the Bishop of Ely to compel Dr Walker to
act ; then, for a writ to compel the Bishop to do his own
duty as General Visitor.   All in vain.   On April 22,
1738, the Court rejected the last of these applications.

That day marks the end of the strife begun in February, 1710 : it had thus lasted a year longer than the
Peloponnesian War.   It has two main chapters.   The
first is the fourteen years' struggle from 1710 to 1724,
in which Miller was the leader down to his withdrawal
in 1719.   The years 1725—1727 were a pause.   Then
the ten years' struggle, from 1728 to 1738, was organised
and maintained by Colbatch.   Meanwhile many of the
persons concerned were advanced in age.   Three weeks
after the King's Bench had refused the third mandamus,
Bishop Greene died at the age of eighty.   Dr Colbatch
was seventy-five.   Bentley himself was seventy-seven.
If he had wanted another classical theme for the candi-

dates in the scholarship examination, he might have
given them—'*One man by his delay hath restored our
fortunes.*' He was under sentence of deprivation, but
only one person could statutably deprive him; that
person declined to move; and no one could make him
move. Bentley therefore remained master of the field—
and of the College.

We remember the incorrigible old gentleman in the
play, whose habit of litigation was so strong that,
when precluded from further attendance on the public
law-courts, he got up a little law-court at home, and
prosecuted his dog. Bentley's occupation with the
King's Bench ceased in April, 1738. In July he
proceeded against Dr Colbatch at Cambridge in the
Consistorial Court of the Bishop of Ely, for the re-
covery of certain payments called 'proxies,' alleged to be
due from Colbatch, as Rector of Orwell, to Bentley, as
Archdeacon of the diocese. The process lasted eighteen
months, at the end of which Dr Colbatch had to pay six
years' arrears and costs.

Looking back on Bentley's long war with the Fellows,
one asks, Who was most to blame? De Quincey approves
Dr Parr's opinion,—expressed long after Bentley's
death,—that the College was wrong, and Bentley right.
But De Quincey goes further. Even granting that
Bentley was wrong, De Quincey says, we ought to vote
him right, 'for by this means the current of one's
sympathy with an illustrious man is cleared of ugly
obstructions.' It is good to be in sympathy with an
illustrious man, but it is better still to be just.
The merits of the controversy between Bentley and
the Fellows have two aspects, legal and moral. The
legal question is simple. Had Bentley, as Master,

brought himself within the meaning of the fortieth
Elizabethan Statute, and deserved the penalty of deprivation? Certainly he had. It was so found on
two distinct occasions, twenty years apart, after a
prolonged investigation by lawyers. Morally, the first
question is: Was Bentley obliged to break the Statutes in order to keep some higher law? He certainly
was not. It cannot be shown that the Statutes
were in conflict with any project which he entertained
for the good of the College; and, if they had been so,
the proper course for him was not to violate them, but
to move constitutionally for their alteration. A further
moral question concerns the nature of his personal
conduct towards the Fellows. This conduct might
conceivably have been so disinterested and considerate
as to give him some equitable claim on their forbearance,
though they might feel bound to resist the course which
he pursued. His conduct was, in fact, of an opposite
character. On a broad view of the whole matter, from
1710 to 1738, the result is this. Legally, the College had
been right, and Bentley wrong. Morally, there had
been faults on both parts; but it was Bentley's intol-
erable behaviour which first, and after long forbearance,
forced the Fellows into an active defence of the common
interests. The words 'Farewell peace to Trinity College'
were pronounced by Bentley. It is not a relevant plea
that his academic ideal was higher than that of the men
whose rights he attacked.

The College necessarily suffered for a time from
these long years of domestic strife which had become a
public scandal. Almost any other society, perhaps,
would have been permanently injured. But Trinity
College had the strength of unique traditions, deeply

rooted in the history of the country ; and the excellent spirit shown by its best men, in the time which immediately followed Bentley's, soon dispelled the cloud. When the grave had closed over those feuds, the good which Bentley had done lived in better tests of merit, and in the traditional association of the College with the encouragement of rising sciences.

Now we must turn to an altogether different side which, throughout these stormy years, is presented by the activity of this extraordinary man.

CHAPTER VIII.

FROM the beginning of 1700 to the summer of 1702 Bentley was constantly occupied with University or College affairs. On August 2, 1702, he writes to Graevius at Utrecht : 'You must know that for the last two years I have hardly had two days free for literature.' This was perhaps the longest decisive interruption of literary work in his whole life. Nearly all his subsequent writings were finished in haste, and many of them were so timed as to appear at moments when he had a special reason for wishing to enlist sympathy. But his studies, as distinguished from his acts of composition, appear to have been seldom broken off for more than short spaces, even when he was most harassed by external troubles. His wonderful nerve and will enabled him to concentrate his spare hours on his own reading, at times when other men would have been able to think of nothing but threatened ruin.

His early years at Trinity College offer several instances of his generous readiness to help and encourage other scholars. One of these was Ludolph Küster, a young Westphalian then living at Cambridge, whom Bentley assisted with an edition of the Greek lexicographer Suidas, and afterwards with an edition of Aristophanes. Another was a young Dutchman, destined to celebrity,—Tiberius Hemsterhuys. Bentley had sent him a kindly criticism on an edition of Julius Pollux, pointing out certain defects of metrical knowledge. The effect on Hemsterhuys has been described by his famous pupil, David Ruhnken. At first he was plunged in despair : then he roused himself to intense effort. To his dying day he revered Bentley, and would hear nothing against him. The story recalls that of F. Jacobs, the editor of the Greek Anthology, who was spurred into closer study of metre by the censures of Godfrey Hermann. In 1709 John Davies, Fellow of Queens' College, Cambridge, published an edition of Cicero's 'Tusculan Disputations,' with an appendix of critical notes by Bentley. The notes were disparaged in a review called the *Bibliothèque Choisie* by the Swiss John Le Clerc, then leader of the Arminians in Holland ; a versatile but shallow man, who had touched the surface of philosophy, and was now ambitious of figuring on the surface of classical literature. Some months later Le Clerc edited the fragments of the Greek comic poets, Menander and Philemon. Nettled by the review, Bentley wrote his own emendations on 323 of these fragments. He restored them metrically, showing that Le Clerc had mixed them with words from the prose texts in which they occur, and had then cut the compound into lengths of twelve syllables, regardless of scansion. Bentley's manuscript, under the name of 'Phileleutherus Lipsiensis,' was transmitted to a scholar at Utrecht, Peter Burmann, who willingly used the permission to publish it. The first edition was sold in three weeks. Le Clerc learned who 'Phileleutherus' was, and wrote a violent letter to

Bentley. Bentley made a caustic reply. He has been
charged with denying the authorship. He does not do
so : but he shows a mischievous pleasure in puzzling his
furious correspondent.

As early as 1702 Bentley had been meditating an
edition of Horace. I translate from his Latin preface
his own account of the motive.

'When, a few years ago [*i. e.* in 1700] I was promoted
to a station in which official duties and harassing cares,
daily surging about me, had distracted me from all deeper
studies, I resolved—in order that I might not wholly
forget the Muses and my old loves—to set about editing
some writer of the pleasanter sort, comparatively light in
style and matter, such as would make in me, rather than
claim from me, a calm and untroubled mind; a work that
could be done bit by bit at odd hours, and would brook
a thousand interruptions without serious loss.   My
choice was HORACE; not because I deemed that I could
restore and correct more things in him than in almost
any other Latin or Greek author; but because he, above
all the ancients—thanks to his merit, or to a peculiar
genius and gift for pleasing—was familiar to men's
hands and hearts.   The form and scope of my work I
defined and limited thus;—that I should touch only
those things which concern the soundness and purity of.
the *text;* but should wholly pass by the mass of those
things which relate to history and ancient manners,—
that vast domain and laboratory of *comment.*'

Bentley began printing his Horace, with his own emendations embodied in the text and the common readings
given at the foot of the page, before he had written the
critical notes which were to justify these changes.   In
August, 1706, he says :—'I have printed three new

sheets in it this last fortnight, and I hope shall go on to
finish by next spring.' Sinister auguries were already
heard in certain quarters. 'I do not wonder,' he writes
to a friend, 'that some...do talk so wildly about my
Horace...I am assured none of them will write against
my notes. They have had enough of me, and will here-
after let me alone.' The rumour of Bentley's new
labours inspired his old enemy, Dr King, with a satire
called 'Horace in Trinity College.' Horace is supposed to
have fulfilled his dream of visiting our remote island
(*visam Britannos*), but to have lost the airy form in
which he proposed to make that excursion,—under the
influence of solid cheer supplied to him from the butteries
of Trinity College.

Instead of appearing in the spring of 1707, Bentley's
Horace was not ready till December 8, 1711. The
summer months were the only part of the year in which
he could do much; and from his preface it would appear
that between 1702 and 1711 there had been four summers
in which he made no progress. The notes on the text
fill 448 quarto pages of small print, in double column,
at the end of the volume. It is characteristic of Bentley
that a great part of these notes were written in about
five months—July to November, 1711. He says himself
that his work was thrown off 'in the first impetus and
glow' of his thoughts, and sent to the press almost before
the ink was dry. It was rather his way to brag of this;
but it must be literally true, to a great extent, of the
notes. He had his own reasons for haste, and worked
at high pressure. The Horace was to be an offering
to Harley, who just then was the umpire of Bentley's
fortunes. In the dedication to the Tory Premier, Bentley
openly announces himself as a converted Whig, by saying

that Maecenas did not like Horace the less for having
borne arms with Brutus and Cassius; not a very happy
allusion, when one remembers that the poet ran away at
Philippi.

Bentley's Horace is a monumental proof of his
ingenuity, learning, and argumentative skill. The notes
abound in hints on grammar and metre which have
a general value. In reading them one feels, too, the
'impetus and glow' of which their author speaks: one
feels almost everywhere the powerful genius of the man.
But while the Horace shows Bentley's critical method on
a large scale and in a most striking form, it illustrates
his defects as conspicuously as his strength. Bentley
had first displayed his skill by restoring deeply corrupted
passages of Greek writers, especially poets. Heroic
remedies were required there. With his wide reading,
unrivalled metrical knowledge, and keen insight, Bentley
had been able to make some restorations which seemed
little of short miraculous. Hopeless nonsense, under
his touch, became lucid and coherent. The applause
which followed these efforts exalted his confidence in his
own gift of divination. His mind was confirmed in a bent
which kept him constantly on the look-out for possible improvements of word or phrase in everything that he read.

Now, Horace was one of the most perilous subjects
that Bentley could have chosen. Not so much because
the text of Horace, as we have it, is particularly
pure. There are many places in which corruption is
certain, and conjecture is the only resource. But, owing
to his peculiar cast of mind and style, Horace is one
of the very last authors whose text should be touched
without absolute necessity. In the Satires and Epistles
his language is coloured by two main influences, subtly

interfused, each of which is very difficult, often impossible, for a modern reader to seize. One is the colloquial idiom of Roman society. The other is literary association, derived from sources, old Italian or Greek, which in many cases are lost. In the Odes, the second of these two influences is naturally predominant; and in them the danger of tampering is more obvious, though perhaps not really greater, than in the Satires or Epistles. Now, Bentley's tendency was to try Horace by the tests of clear syntax, strict logic, and normal usage. He was bent on making Horace 'sound' in a sense less fine, but even more rigorous, than that in which Pope is 'correct.'

Thus, in the 'Art of Poetry,' Horace is speaking of a critic :—'If you told him, *after two or three vain attempts,* that you could not do better, he would bid you erase your work, and put your *ill-turned verses on the anvil* again' (*et male tornatos incudi reddere versus*). 'Ill-turned' —'anvil'! said Bentley : 'what has a lathe to do with an anvil ?' And so, for *male tornatos,* he writes *male ter natos,* 'thrice shaped amiss.' Horace elsewhere speaks of verses as *incultis...et male natis.* To Bentley's reading, however, it may be objected that the order of words required by the sense is *ter male natos* : for *male ter natos* ought to mean, either 'unhappily thrice-born'—like the soul of a Pythagorean, unfortunate in two migrations; or 'barely thrice-born'—as if, in some process which required three refinements, the third was scarcely completed. And then, if we are not satisfied with the simplest account of *tornatos*—viz., that Horace lapsed into a mixture of common metaphors—it admits of a strict defence. The verses have been put on the lathe, but have not been successfully rounded and polished. Then, says Horace's critic, they must go back to the

anvil, and be forged anew, passing again through that first
process by which the rough material is brought into shape
for the lathe. Yet Bentley was so sure of his *ter natos* that
persons who doubted it seemed no better than ' moles.'

Another instance will illustrate the danger of altering
touches in Horace which may have been suggested by
some lost literary source. In the Odes (III. iv. 45)
Horace speaks of Jupiter as ruling '*cities* and troubled
realms, and gods, and *the multitudes of men*' (urbes...
mortalisque turbas). 'Tell me, pray,' cries Bentley,
'what is the sense of 'cities' and 'the multitudes
of men' ? This is silly—mere tautology.' And so he
changes *urbes*, 'cities,' into *umbras*, 'the shades' of the
departed. Now, as Munro has pointed out, Horace
may have had in mind a passage in the *Epicharmus*,
a philosophical poem by Ennius, of which a few lines
remain : where it is said of Jupiter, '*mortalis atque urbes*
beluasque omnes iuvat.' One or two of Bentley's
corrections are not only admirable but almost certain
(as *musto* Falerno for *misto* in the Satires II. iv. 19). A
few more have reason wholly on their side, and yet are
not intrinsically probable. Thus in the Epistles (I. vii. 29)
we have the fable of the fox, who, when lean, crept
through a chink into a granary, and there grew too fat
to get out again. 'To the rescue,' exclaims Bentley,
'ye sportsmen, rustics, and naturalists ! A fox eating
grain !' And so Bentley changes the fox into a field-
mouse (*volpecula* into *nitedula*). But the old fabulist
from whom Horace got the story, meaning to show how
cunning greed may overreach itself, had chosen the
animal which is the type of cunning, without thinking of
the points on which Bentley dwells, the structure of its
teeth and its digestive organs.

Bentley has made altogether between 700 and 800
changes in the text of Horace : in his preface, he recalls
19 of these, but adds a new one (*rectis* oculis for *siccis* in
Odes I. iii. 18 : which convinced Porson).   His paramount
guide, he declares, has been his own faculty of divination.
To this, he says, he has owed more corrections, and corrections of greater certainty, than to the manuscripts,—in
using which, however, where he does use them, he nearly
always shows the greatest tact.   Now, criticism of a text
has only one proper object—to exhibit what the author
wrote.   It is a different thing to show what he might
have written.   Bentley's passion for the exercise of his
divining faculty hindered him from keeping this simple
fact clearly before his mind.   In the 'Art of Poetry' (60)
Horace has : *Ut silvae foliis pronos mutantur in annos :*
'As woods suffer change of leaves with each declining
year.'   Nothing could be less open to suspicion,—*foliis*
being an ordinary ablative of the part affected (like
capti auribus et oculis for 'deaf and blind').   Yet Bentley
must needs change this good line into one which is
bad both in style and in metre :—*Ut silvis folia privos
mutantur in annos,* 'as woods have their leaves changed
with each year' ; and this he prints in his text.   Speaking of Bentley's readings in the mass, one may say that
Horace would probably have liked two or three of them,—
would have allowed a very few more as not much better
or worse than his own,—and would have rejected the
immense majority with a smile or a shudder.

On the other hand, there is a larger sense in which
Bentley's Horace is a model of conservative prudence.
Recent German criticism has inclined to the view that
Horace's works are interpolated not only with spurious
passages but with whole spurious poems.   Thus Mr O.

F. Gruppe actually rejects the whole of the beautiful ode,
Tyrrhena regum progenies (III. xxix.). Another critic,
Mr Hofmann-Peerlkamp, regrets that Bentley's haste
blinded him to many interpolations. Haupt, Meineke,
Ritschl have favoured the same tendency. The prevail-
ing view of English scholarship is that the solitary
interpolation in our Horace consists of the eight lines
(*Lucili, quam sis mendosus* &c.) prefixed to Satire I. 10,
and probably as old, or nearly so, as the poem itself.
Bentley's suspicions are confined to a few single lines
here and there. But there is only one line in all Horace
which he positively condemns. It is mainly a point
of literary criticism, and is a curious example of his
method. I give it in Latin and English (Odes IV.
viii. 15) :—

Non celeres fugae
Reiectaeque retrorsum Hannibalis minae,
Non incendia Carthaginis impiae
Eius qui domita nomen ab Africa
Lucratus rediit clarius indicant
Laudes, quam Calabrae Pierides...

Not the swift flight
And menace backward hurled of Hannibal,
Not impious Carthage sinking into fire
So well gives forth his praises, who returned
With title won from conquered Africa,
As ye, Calabria's Muses...

Now, says Bentley, the Scipio (Africanus maior)
who defeated Hannibal in the Second Punic War is a
different person from the Scipio (Africanus minor)
who burned Carthage more than half a century later.
How can it be said that the defeat of Hannibal glorifies
the destroyer of Carthage? And so Bentley would leave
out the burning of Carthage, and make the whole passage

refer to the conqueror of Hannibal. The answer seems
plain. Horace means : 'The glory of the Scipios never
reached a higher pinnacle than that on which it was placed
by the Calabrian poet Ennius, when he described the defeat of Hannibal by the elder Africanus ; though that
achievement was crowned by the younger Africanus,
when he finally destroyed Carthage.' The 'praises' of
the younger Africanus are not exclusively his personal
exploits, but the glories, both ancestral and personal,
of his name. Then Bentley objects to the caesura in
Non incendia Carth|aginis impiae. But what of the
undoubtedly genuine verse, *Dum flagrantia de|torquet
ad oscula* (Odes ii. xii. 25)? 'The preposition *de*,' he
replies, 'is, as it were, separated from the verb *torquet*,—
not being a native part of that word.' This might
seem a bold plea ; but it shows his knowledge. In old
Latin inscriptions the preposition and the rest of the
word are often disjoined,—for instance, IN VICTO could
stand for INVICTO : and Bentley's principle would apply
to Horace's *Arcanique fides prodiga per|lucidior vitro*
(Odes i. xviii. 16). If, however, *Carthaginis* has not
the privilege of a compound, it may have that of a
proper name. The presence of a proper name has been
urged in excuse of *Mentemque lymphat|am Mareotico*
(Od. i. xxxvii. 14), *Spectandus in cert|amine Martio*
(Od. iv. xiv. 17). Bentley does not notice this ground
of defence. Finally, he rejects 'Non incendia Carthaginis impiae' as a verse of 'manifestly monkish spirit
and colour.'

Bentley was the first modern editor who followed the
best ancient authorities in calling the Odes *Carmina* and
not *Odae*, the Satires *Sermones* and not *Satirae*. In his
preface he endeavours to settle the chronological order of

Horace's writings. Previous Horatian critics—as Faber,
Dacier, Masson—had aimed at dating separate poems.
Bentley maintains—rightly, no doubt—that the poems
were originally *published*, as we have them, in whole
books. He further assumes—with much less probability—
that Horace *composed* in only one style at a time, first
writing satires; then iambics (the 'Epodes'); then the
Odes,—of which book IV. and the Carmen Saeculare
came between the two books of Epistles. Bentley's
method is too rigid. He argues from the internal
evidence too much as if a poet's works were the successive
numbers of a newspaper. Yet here, too,—though some
of his particular views are arbitrary or wrong,—he laid
down the main lines of a true scheme.

Bentley's Horace immediately brought out half-a-
dozen squibs,—none of them good,—and one or two more
serious attacks. John Ker, a schoolmaster, assailed
Bentley's Latinity in four Letters (1713); and some
years later the same ground was taken by Richard
Johnson—who had been a contemporary of Bentley's at
Cambridge, and was now master of Nottingham School—
in his *Aristarchus Anti-Bentleianus* (1717). The fact is
that Bentley wrote Latin as he wrote English,—with
racy vigour, and with a wealth of trenchant phrases;
but he was not minutely Ciceronian. The two critics
were able to pick some holes. One of Bentley's
slips was amusing; he promises the readers of his
Horace that they will find purity of idiom in his
Latin notes,—and calls it *sermonis puritatem*—which
happens *not* to be pure Latin. In 1721 a rival Horace
was published by Alexander Cunningham, a Scottish
scholar of great learning and industry. His emendations
are sometimes execrable, but often most ingenious. His

work is marred, however, by a mean spite against Bentley, whom he constantly tries to represent as a plagiarist or a blunderer,—and who ignored him.

The first edition of Bentley's Horace (1711) went off rapidly, and a second was required in 1712. This was published by the eminent firm of Wetstein at Amsterdam. Paper and printing were cheaper there—an important point when the book was to reach all scholars. Thomas Bentley, the nephew, brought out a smaller edition of the work in 1713, dedicating it—with logical propriety—to Harley's *son*. The line in the *Dunciad* (II. 205),—' Bentley his mouth with classic flatt'ry opes,' —is fixed by Warburton on Thomas Bentley, ' a small critic, who aped his uncle in a little Horace.' Among other compliments, Bentley received one or two which he could scarcely have anticipated. Le Clerc, whom he had just been lashing so unmercifully, wrote a review in the *Bibliothèque Choisie* which was at once generous and judicious. Bentley also received a graceful note from Atterbury, now Dean of Christ Church. ' I am indebted to you, Sir,' says the Dean, ' for the great pleasure and instruction I have received from that excellent performance; though at y⁰ same time I cannot but own to you the uneasyness I felt when I found how many things in Horace there were, which, after thirty years' acquaintance with him, I did not understand.' There is much of Horace in that.

CHAPTER IX.

ONE of Bentley's few intimate friends in the second
half of his life was Dr Richard Mead, an eminent
physician, and in other ways also a remarkable man.
After graduating at the University of Padua,—which,
as Cambridge men will remember, had been the second
alma mater of Dr John Caius,—Dr Mead began practice
at Stepney in 1696. He rose rapidly to the front
rank of his profession, in which he stood from about
1720 to his death in 1754. Dibdin describes him with
quaint enthusiasm. 'His house was the general re-
ceptacle of men of genius and talent, and of everything
beautiful, precious or rare. His curiosities, whether
books, or coins, or pictures, were laid open to the public;
and the enterprising student and experienced antiquary
alike found amusement and a courteous reception. He
was known to all foreigners of intellectual distinction, and
corresponded both with the artisan and the potentate.'

In 1721—Bentley being in London at the time—
Mead gave him a copy of a Greek inscription just
published by the accomplished antiquary, Edmund
Chishull, who had been chaplain to the English Factory

at Smyrna. A marble slab, about 8 feet 7 inches high
and 18 inches broad, had been found in the Troad. It
is now in the British Museum. This slab had supported
the bust of a person who had presented some pieces of
plate to the citizens of Sigeum; on the upper part, an
inscription in Ionic Greek records the gifts; lower down,
nearly the same words are repeated in Attic Greek, with
the addition,—'Aesopus and his brothers made me.'
Bentley dashed off a letter to Mead; there had been no
bust at all, he said; the two inscriptions on the slab were
merely copied from two of the pieces of plate; the artists
named were the silversmiths. He was mistaken. The
true solution is clearly that which has since been given
by Kirchhoff. The Ionic inscription was first carved by
order of the donor, a native of the Ionic Proconnesus:
the lower inscription was added at Sigeum, where
settlers had introduced the Attic dialect, on its being
found that the upper inscription could not easily be read
from beneath: Aesopus and his brothers were the stone-
cutters. Yet Bentley's letter incidentally throws a flash
of light on a point not belonging to its main subject.
A colossal statue of Apollo had been dedicated in Delos
by the islanders of Naxos. On the base are these
words :—ΟϜΥΤΟΛΙΘΟΕΜΙΑΝΔΡΙΑΣΚΑΙΤΟΣΦΕΛΑΣ. Bentley read
this (τ)οϜυτοῦ [= ταὐτοῦ] λίθου εἴμ', ἀνδριὰς καὶ τὸ σφέλας,
an iambic trimeter (with hiatus) : 'I am of the same
stone, statue and pedestal.'

After this instance of rashness, it is right to record
a striking success. In 1728 Chishull published an inscription from copies made by the travellers Spon and
Wheeler. Bentley, in a private letter, suggested some
corrections; but Chishull, who saw the criticisms without knowing the author, demurred to some of them,

thinking that the copies could not have been so in-
exact. Some years later the stone itself was brought
to England. It then appeared that the copies had been
wrong, and that Bentley's conjectural reading agreed in
every particular with the marble itself. That marble
is in the British Museum : it was found at the ancient
Chalcedon on the Bosporus, opposite Constantinople, and
had supported a statue of *Zeus Ourios*, i.e. 'Zeus the
giver of fair winds.' He had a famous temple in that
neighbourhood, at the mouth of the Black Sea, where
voyagers thròugh the straits were wont to make their
vows. The inscription (3797 in the *Corpus*) consists of
four elegiac couplets, of which the style would justify
us in supposing that they were at least as old as the
age of Alexander : I translate them :—

> Zeus, the sure guide who sends the favouring gale,
> Claims a last vow before ye spread the sail :
> If to the Azure Rocks your course ye urge,
> Where in the strait Poseidon lifts the surge,
> Or through the broad Ægean seek your home,
> Here lay your gift—and speed across the foam.
> Behold the god, whose wafting breath divine
> All mortals welcome : Philon raised the sign.

It was shortly before his death in 1742 that this
proof of his acuteness was given to the world (by John
Taylor), along with another. A Persian manuscript bore
the date '*Yonane* (Ionian) 1504': Bentley showed that
this was reckoned from the foundation of the dynasty
of Seleucidae—'Ionian' being the general oriental name
for 'Hellene'—and meant the year 1193 of our era.

In 1724 an edition of Terence was published by Dr
Francis Hare. Bentley had long meditated such a work.
He was never a jealous man. But he had a good deal of

the feeling expressed by the verse, 'Shame to be mute and let barbarians speak.' He put forth all his powers. At the beginning of 1726—that is, some eighteen months after the appearance of Hare's Terence—Bentley's came out. And it was not Terence only. Hare had promised the Fables of Phaedrus, and Bentley forestalled him by giving these in the same volume; also the 'Sentences' (273 lines) of the so-called Publius Syrus.

The Terence is one of Bentley's titles to fame. Any attempt to criticise such an author's text demands a knowledge of his metres. Bentley was the first modern who threw any clear light on the metrical system of the Latin dramatists. Here, as in other cases, it is essential to remember the point at which he took up the work. Little or nothing of scientific value had been done before him. The prevalent view had been based on that of Priscian, who recognised in Terence only two metres, the iambic and the trochaic,—the metre of which the basis is ⏑ –, and that of which it is – ⏑. Every verse was to be forced into one or other of these moulds, by assuming all manner of 'licences' on the part of the poet. Nay, Priscian says that in his time some persons denied that there were any metres in Terence at all! (*quosdam vel abnegare esse in Terentii comoediis metra*). In the preface to an edition of Terence which appeared almost simultaneously with Bentley's, the Dutch editor, Westerhof, alludes ironically to a hint in Bentley's Horace (Sat. II. v. 79) that it was possible to restore the Terentian metres; a sneer which it was Westerhof's fate to expiate by compiling the index for Bentley's second edition when it was published at Amsterdam in 1727. The scholars of the sixteenth century who had treated the subject—Glareanus, Erasmus, Faernus—had followed the 'licence' theory. Bentley's object was to reclaim as much as possible from this supposed realm of 'licence,' and enlarge the domain of law. He points out, first, the variety of Terence's metres, and illustrates each by an English verse. He then defines certain metrical differences between Roman Comedy, as in Terence, and Roman epic poetry, as in Virgil. The characteristic of Bentley's views on Terentian metre consisted in taking account of accent ('prosody' in the proper sense), and not solely of quantity. To judge from some of Bentley's emendations in poetry, his ear for sound was not very fine ; but his ear for rhythm was exact. Guided by this, he could see that the influence of accent in Roman Comedy sometimes overruled the epic and lyric canons of quantitative metre. In one case, however, his attention to accent led him into an erroneous refinement. In Latin, he says, no word of two or more syllables is accented on the last syllable : thus it is *vírum*, not *virúm*. Comic poets, he urges, writing for popular audiences, had to guard as much as possible against laying a metrical stress on these final syllables which could not support an accent. In the iambic trimeter they could not observe this rule everywhere. But Terence, said Bentley, always observes it in the third foot. As an example, I may take this verse:—

Ultro ád | me ven'|it ún|icam || gnatám | suam :

where the rule, though broken in the 5th foot, is kept in the 3rd. But Bentley seems not to have noticed that this is a result of metre, not of accent : it is due to the caesura.

Bentley corrected the text of Terence in about a thousand places ('mille, opinor, locis,' he says),—chiefly on metrical grounds. Yet in every scene of every play, according to Ritschl, he left serious blemishes. That only shows what was the state of the field in which Bentley broke new ground. His work must not be judged as if he propounded a complete metrical doctrine. Rather he threw out a series of original remarks, right in some points, wrong in others, pregnant in all. G. Hermann and Ritschl necessarily speak of Bentley's labours on Terence with mingled praise and censure; both, however, do full justice to the true instinct with which he led the attack on the problem. Modern studies in Latin metre and pronunciation have advanced the questions treated by Bentley to a new stage; but his merit remains. He was the pioneer of metrical knowledge in its application to the Latin drama.

A word of mention is due to the very curious Latin speech which Bentley has printed in his Terence after the sketch of the metres. It was delivered by him on July 6, 1725, when, as Regius Professor of Divinity, he had occasion to present seven incepting doctors in that faculty. He interprets the old symbols of the doctoral degree,—the cap,—the book,—the gold ring,—the chair ('believe those who have tried it—no bench is so hard');— and congratulates the University on the beneficence of George I. It has been wondered why Bentley inserted this speech in his Terence. Surely the reason is evident. He had recently been restored to those degrees which had been taken from him by the Cambridge Senate in 1718. He seizes this opportunity of intimating to the world that he is once more in full exercise of his functions as Regius Professor of Divinity.

It was in his seventy-seventh year (1739) that Bentley fulfilled a project of his youth by publishing an

edition of Manilius. At the age of twenty-nine (1691)
he had been actively collecting materials, and had even
made some progress with the text. In 1727 we find that
this work, so long laid aside, stood first on the list of
promises to be redeemed : and in 1736 it was ready for
press. A proposal for publishing it was made to Bentley
by a London 'Society for the Encouragement of Learning,'
which aimed at protecting authors from booksellers.
Bentley declined. The Manilius was printed in 1739 by
Henry Woodfall. It is a beautiful quarto ; the frontispiece is Vertue's engraving of Thornhill's portrait of
Bentley, *aetat.* 48 (1710) ; a good engraving, though a
conventional benignity tames and spoils that peculiar
expression which is so striking in the picture at Trinity
College.

Manilius is the author of an epic poem in five books,
called *Astronomica:* but popular astronomy is subordinate,
in his treatment, to astrology. Strangely enough, the
poet's age was so open a question with the scholars of
the seventeenth century that Gevärts actually identified
him with Theodorus Mallius, consul in 399 A.D., whom
Claudian panegyrises. The preface to Bentley's edition,
written by his nephew Richard, rightly assigns Manilius
to the age of Augustus, though without giving the internal proofs. These are plain. Book I. was finished after
the defeat of Varus (A.D. 9), and Book IV. before the
death of Augustus (A.D. 14). F. Jacob, in his edition of
the poet (rec. Berlin 1846), understands a verse in Book
V. (512) as referring to the restoration by Tiberius of
Pompey's Theatre, after it had been burnt down in 22
A.D. But, according to the marble of Ancyra, Augustus
also had repaired that theatre at a great cost, and took
credit for allowing the name of Pompey to remain in the

dedicatory inscription, instead of replacing it by his own.
Clearly it is to this that the words of Manilius allude,—
Hinc Pompeia manent veteris monimenta triumphi,—
implying a compliment not only to the munificence, but
to the magnanimity, of Augustus. There is no reason,
then, for doubting that the whole poem was composed,
or took its present shape, between A. D. 9 and A. D. 14.
The poet gives no clue to his own origin, but his style
has a strongly Greek tinge.

Scaliger pronounced him 'equal in sweetness to Ovid,
and superior in majesty;' a verdict which Bentley cites
with approval. To most readers it will be scarcely in-
telligible. Where Manilius deals with the technical
parts of astronomy, he displays, indeed, excellent ingenuity; but, in the frequent passages where he imitates
Lucretius, the contrast between a poet and a rhetorician
is made only more glaring by an archaic diction. The
episode of Andromeda and Perseus, in his fifth book, and
a passage on human reason in the second, were once
greatly admired. To show him at his best, however,
I should rather take one of those places where he expresses more simply a feeling of wonder and awe common to every age. ' *Wherefore see we the stars arise in
their seasons, and move, as at a word spoken, on the
paths appointed for them? Of whom there is none
that hastens, neither is there any that tarries behind.
Why are the summer nights beautiful with these that
change not, and the nights of winter from of old? These
things are not the work of chance, but the order of a God
most high.*'

Bentley's treatment of the text sometimes exhibits
all his brilliancy: thus in Book v. 737 the received
text had—

Sic etiam magno quaedam respondere mundo
Haec Natura facit, quae *caeli* condidit orbem.

This *respondĕre* had even been quoted to show that
the poem was post-classical. The MSS. have not *Haec*,
but QUAM : not *caeli* but CAELO : and one good MS. has
MUNDO EST. Bentley restores :—

Sic etiam in magno quaedam RESPUBLICA mundo est,
Quam Natura facit, quae caelo condidit URBEM.

'So also in the great firmament there is a commonwealth,
wrought by Nature, who hath ordered a city in the
heavens.' *Respondere* arose from a contraction *resp.*
And *urbem* is made certain by the next verses, which
elaborate the comparison of the starry hierarchy to the
various ranks of civic life. But this, Bentley's last
published work, shows a tendency from which his earlier
criticism was comparatively free. Not content with
amending, he rejects very many verses as spurious. The
total number is no less than 170 out of 4220 lines which
the poem contains. In the vast majority of cases, the
ground of rejection is wholly and obviously inadequate.
As an example of his rashness here, we may take
one passage,—which, I venture to think, he has not understood. At the beginning of Book IV. Manilius is reciting
the glories of Rome.

Quid referam Cannas admotaque moenibus arma?
Varronemque fuga magnum (quod vivere possit
Postque tuos, Thrasimene, lacus) Fabiumque morando?
Accepisse iugum victas Carthaginis arces?

'Why should I tell of Cannae, and of (Carthaginian) arms
carried to the walls of Rome? Why tell of Varro, great in his
flight, ... and Fabius, in his delay? Or how the conquered
towers of Carthage received our yoke?'

Varro's 'flight' is his escape from the field of Cannae,

after which he saved the remnant of the Roman army. The words, *quod vivere possit Postque tuos, Thrasimene, lacus*, are untranslateable. Bentley seems to have understood :—'in that he can live, and that, too, after the battle at Lake Thrasimene :' but, to say no more, *que* forbids this. And then he rejects the whole line, *Accepisse—arces.* Why ? Because 'yokes' are put on peoples, not on 'towers'! Now the oldest manuscript (Gemblacensis) has not *vivere*, but VINCERE : the MSS. have not *quod* (a conjecture), but QUAM. They have also MORANTEM (not *morando*), VICTAE (not *victas*). I should read :—

Quid referam Cannas admotaque moenibus arma ?
Varronemque fuga magnum, Fabiumque morantem ?
Postque tuos, Thrasimene, lacus QUOM VINCERE POSSET,
Accepisse iugum victae Carthaginis arces ?

'and that,—though after the fight by thy waters, Thrasimene, she could hope to conquer,—the towers of conquered Carthage received our yoke.'

The words 'quom vincere posset' allude to the imminent peril of Rome after Hannibal's great victory at Lake Thrasimene, when the fall of the city seemed inevitable if the conqueror should march upon it. (Cp. Liv. XXII. 7 f.)

It remains to speak of another labour which Bentley was not destined to complete, but which, even in its comparatively slight relics, offers points of great interest —his Homer.

The first trace of Homeric criticism by Bentley occurs in a letter which he wrote to his friend Davies, of Queens' College, just after Joshua Barnes had published his edition of the Iliad and Odyssey (1711). Barnes, who was unreasonably offended with Bentley, refers in

his preface to a certain 'hostile person,' a very Zoilus.
'If he mean me,' says Bentley, ' I have but dipped yet
into his notes, and yet I find everywhere just occasion of
censure.' Bentley then shows that Barnes had made an
arbitrary change in a line of the Iliad (αὐτάρ for ἀλλά in
XIV. 101), through not seeing that a reading which had
stood in all former editions, and which had puzzled the
Greek commentator Eustathius, was a mere blunder
(ἀποπτανέουσιν for ἀποπαπτανέουσιν). In 1713 Bentley
published his 'Remarks' on the 'Discourse of Free-
Thinking' by Anthony Collins. Collins had spoken
of the Iliad as 'the epitome of all arts and sciences,'
adding that Homer 'designed his poem for eternity,
to please and instruct mankind.' 'Take my word for
it,' says Bentley, 'poor Homer, in those circumstances
and early times, had never such aspiring thoughts. He
wrote a sequel of songs and rhapsodies, to be sung by
himself for small earnings and good cheer, at festivals
and other days of merriment; the *Ilias* he made for the
men, and the *Odysseïs* for the other sex. These loose
songs were not collected together in the form of an epic
poem till Pisistratus's time, above [2nd edition: 1st,
about] 500 years after.' There is some ambiguity in the
phrase, 'a *sequel* of songs and rhapsodies.' It seems
improbable that Bentley meant, ' a *connected* series.'

When Bentley wrote this, the origin of the Homeric
poems had not yet become a subject of modern controversy. It would be unfair to press his casual utterance
as if it were a carefully defined statement. Yet it is
interesting to note the general outlines of the belief
which satisfied a mind so bold and so acute. He
supposes, then, that a poet named Homer lived about
1050 B. C. This poet 'wrote' (by which, perhaps, he

meant no more than 'composed') both the Iliad and
the Odyssey. But neither of them was given to the
world by Homer as a single epic. Each consisted
of many short lays, which Homer recited separately.
These lays circulated merely as detached pieces, until
they were collected about 550 B. C. into the two epics
which we possess.

Seventy-two years later F. A. Wolf published his
Prolegomena. The early epic poetry of Greece, Wolf
argues, was transmitted by oral recitation, not by
writing. But *our* Iliad and Odyssey could not have
been composed without writing. We must conclude,
then, that the Homeric poems were originally, in
Bentley's phrase, 'a sequel of songs and rhapsodies.'
These 'loose songs' were first written down and arranged by the care of Peisistratus. Thus Bentley's
sentence contains the germ of the view which Wolf
developed. Yet it would be an error to conceive Bentley
here as an original sceptic, who threw out the first
pregnant hint of a new theory. Bentley's relation to
the modern Homeric question is of a different kind.
The view which he expresses was directly derived by him
from notices in ancient writers; as when Pausanias says
that the Homeric poems, before their collection by
Peisistratus, had been 'scattered, and preserved only by
memory, some here, some there.' Cicero, Plutarch,
Diogenes Laertius, the Platonic *Hipparchus,* Heracleides
Ponticus, were other witnesses to whom Bentley could
appeal.

He brought forward and approved that old tradition
at a time when the original unity of each epic was the
received belief. It was not till the latter part of the
eighteenth century that the passion for returning from

'art' to 'nature' prepared a welcome for the doctrine
that the Iliad and the Odyssey are parcels of primitive
folk-songs.   But then we note the off-hand way in which
Bentley's statement assumes points which have since
vexed Homeric research.   He assumes that the Iliad
and Odyssey are made up of parts which were *originally*
intended for detached recitations : an inference to which
the structure of the poems is strongly adverse.   He ac-
cepts without reserve the tradition regarding Peisistratus.
By the ancient saying that the Iliad was written for
men and the Odyssey for women, Bentley probably understood no more than that the Iliad deals with war, and
the Odyssey with the trials of a true wife.   There is,
indeed, a further sense in which we might say that the
Iliad, with its historical spirit, was masculine, and the
Odyssey, with its fairy-land wonders and its tender pathos,
more akin to *das Ewigweibliche :* but we cannot read that
meaning into Bentley's words.   He seems to have found
no such difference between the characters of the two epics
as constrained him to become a 'separator.'   He had not
felt, what is now so generally admitted, that the Odyssey
bears the marks of a later time than the Iliad.   Briefly,
then, we cannot properly regard Bentley as a forerunner
of the Homeric controversy on its literary or historical
side, preeminently as his critical gifts would have fitted
him to take up the question.   He knew the ancient
sources on which Wolf afterwards worked, but he had
not given his mind to sifting them.   Bentley's connec-
tion with Homeric criticism is wholly on the side of the
text, and chiefly in regard to metre.

In 1726 Bentley was meditating an edition of
Homer, but intended first to finish his labours on the
New Testament.   In 1732 he definitely committed him-

self to the Homeric task. At that time the House of
Lords had before it the question whether the Bishop of
Ely could try Bentley. As the Horace had been
dedicated to Harley, so the Homer was to be dedicated
to Lord Carteret, a peer who was favourable to the
Master of Trinity's cause, and who encouraged the design
by granting or procuring the loan of manuscripts. In
1734 we find Bentley at work on Homer. But, though
he made some progress, nothing was published. Trinity
College possesses the only relics of his Homeric work.

First, there is a copy of H. Estienne's folio *Poetae
Graeci*. In this Bentley had read through the Iliad,
Odyssey, and Homeric Hymns, writing very brief notes
in the margin, which are either his own corrections,
or readings from manuscripts or grammarians. In the
Hymns the notes become rarer; and it is evident that
all were written rapidly. This is the book which Trinity
College sent in 1790 to Göttingen, for the use of Heyne,
who warmly acknowledges the benefit in the preface to
his edition of the Iliad. Secondly, a small quarto manuscript book contains somewhat fuller notes by Bentley
on the first six books of the Iliad. These notes occupy
43 pages of the book, ceasing abruptly at verse 54 of
Iliad VII. Lastly, there is the manuscript draft of
Bentley's notes on the digamma, the substance of which
has been published by J. W. Donaldson in his *New
Cratylus*.

The distinctive feature of Bentley's Homeric work is
the restoration of the digamma. Bentley's discovery was
too much in advance of his age to be generally received
otherwise than with ridicule or disbelief. Even F. A. Wolf,
who yielded to few in his admiration of the English critic,
could speak of the digamma as merely an illusion which,

in old age, mocked the genius of Bentley (*senile ludibrium ingenii Bentleiani*). At the present day, when the philological fact has so long been seen in a clearer light, it is easy to underrate the originality and the insight which the first perception of it showed.

In reading Homer, Bentley had been struck by such things as these. The words, '*and Atreides the king*,' are in Homer, *Atreides te anax*. Now the *e* in *te* would naturally be cut off before the first *a* in *anax*, making *t'anax*. But the poet cannot have meant to cut it off, since that would spoil the metre. Why, then, was he able to avoid cutting it off? Because, said Bentley, in Homer's time the word *anax* did not begin with a vowel: it was *vanax*. Many old writers mention a letter which had disappeared from the ordinary Greek alphabet. Its sound had been like the Latin v,—that is, probably, like our w. Its form was like F: which, to Greek eyes, suggested their letter gamma, Γ, with another gamma on its shoulders: and so they called this F the 'double gamma,' the *digamma*. Several words are specified by the old grammarians as having once begun with this digamma. Bentley tried the experiment of replacing it before such words where they occurred in Homer. Very often, he found, this explained a gap (or 'hiatus'), like that in *Atreides te anax*. He came to the conclusion that, when the Homeric poems were composed, this letter was still used, and that it should *always* be prefixed, in Homer, to those words which once had it.

The first hint of this idea occurs in Bentley's copy (now at Trinity College) of the 'Discourse of Free-Thinking' by Anthony Collins, which Bentley was reading and annotating in 1713. On a blank leaf at the end he has written :—

Homer's δίγαμμα Aeolicum to be added. οἶνος, Ϝοῖνος, vinū : a Demonstration of this, because Ϝοῖνος has always preceding it a vowel : so οἰνοποτάζων.

Bentley's view was noticed by his friend Dr Samuel Clarke, in the second volume of his Iliad, published posthumously in 1732. In the same year came forth Bentley's edition of *Paradise Lost*, in which he had occasion to quote Homer. There the digamma makes its modern *début* in all the majesty of a capital F,—for which printers now use the sign Ϝ. It was the odd look of such a word as Ϝέτος that inspired Pope with the lines in the *Dunciad*. Bentley speaks :—

> Roman and Greek grammarians ! know your better,
> Author of something yet more great than letter ;
> While tow'ring o'er your alphabet, like Saul,
> Stands our digamma, and o'ertops them all.

Bentley had thrown a true and brilliant light on the text of Homer. But, as was natural then, he pushed his conclusion too far. The Greek *Foinos* is the same as *vinum* and *wine*. Homer, Bentley thought, could no more have said *oinos*, instead of *voinos*, than Romans could say *inum*, or Englishmen *ine*. Accordingly, he set to work to restore this letter all through the Homeric poems. Often it mended the metre, but not seldom it marred it ; and then Bentley was for changing the text. A single instance will give some idea of his task. In Iliad I. 202 we have the words *hŭbrĭn ĭdē* (ὕβριν ἴδῃ), (that thou mayest) '*see* the *insolence*.' This word *ide* was originally *vide :* its stem *vid* is that of the Latin *video* and our *wit*. Homer, said Bentley, could have written nothing but *vide*. And so, to make the metre right, he reads a different word (ὀρῇς). Now let us see what this involves. This stem *vid* is the parent of several words, very frequent

in Homer, for *seeing, seeming, knowing, form*, etc. On
Bentley's view, every one of these must always, in Homer,
begin with F. The number of changes required can
easily be estimated by anyone who will consult Prender-
gast's Concordance to the Iliad, Dunbar's to the Odyssey
and Homeric Hymns. I do not guarantee the absolute
precision of the following numbers, but they are at least
approximately correct. I find that about 832 derivatives
of the stem *vid* occur in the Iliad, Odyssey, and Hymns.
By F I denote those cases in which the metre *requires*
the digamma: by N, those in which the metre *excludes*
it : by Q, those cases which prove nothing :—

	Total.	F	N	Q
Iliad.........	357	205	81	71
Odyssey ...	376	220	76	80
Hymns	99	38	34	27
	832	463	191	178

So, for this one root *vid*, Bentley would have been
compelled to amend the text of Homer in about 191
places. The number of digammated roots in Homer is
between 30 and 40 ; no other is so prolific as *vid;* but a
consistent restoration of the digamma would require
change in at least several hundreds of places; and often
under conditions which require that the changes, if any,
should be extremely bold. Bentley's error consisted in
regarding the digamma as a constant element, like any
other letter in the radical parts of the words to which
it had once been prefixed. It was not this, but rather
the ghost of a vanished letter, which, in Homeric metre,

fitfully haunts its ancient seats.   Nor is it the only such
ghost.   When Bentley found that, in Homer, the word
ὡς, 'as,' can be treated as if it began with a consonant,
he wrote Ϝώς : but the lost initial was not the spirant
ν : it was γ : for ὡς is merely the ablative of ὅ-ς, the
Sanskrit *yât*.

Apart from the restoration of the digamma, the relics
of Bentley's work on Homer present other attempts at
emendation.   These are always acute and ingenious; but
the instances are rare indeed in which they would now
commend themselves to students.   I give a few specimens
below, in order that scholars may judge of their general
character*.   The boldness with which Bentley was disposed

* I. *From Bentley's MS. notes in the margin of the Homer.*
Odyssey I. 23 ('Αλλ' ὁ μὲν Αἰθίοπας μετεκίαθε τηλόθ' ἐόντας, |
Αἰθίοπας, τοὶ διχθὰ δεδαίαται, ἔσχατοι ἀνδρῶν). ' legendum Αἰθίοπες :
si vera lectio Il. Z. 396.' (θυγάτηρ μεγαλήτορος 'Ηετίωνος, | 'Ηετίων,
ὃς ἔναιεν, κ.τ.λ.) [Lucian speaks of 'Attic solecisms,'—deliberate
imitations, by late writers, of the irregular grammar found in
Attic writers: surely this is a gratuitous 'Homeric solecism.']
29. (μνήσατο γὰρ κατὰ θυμὸν ἀμύμονος Αἰγίσθοιο.) Bentley conjectures κατὰ νοῦν ἀνοήμονος. 51. θεὰ δ' ἐν δώμασι ναίει ' Eust. not.
ἐν δώματα ναίει pro vulg. δώμασι, sed lego θεὰ δ' ἐν πότνια ναίει.
ἐνναίει absolute, ut ἐνναίουσι Il. 1. 154, 296. Sic Od. E. 215 eam
compellens Πότνα θεά. κοὐ δώματα ἔναιεν sed σπέος. Ibidem.' [*i.e.*
Bentley objects to the word δώματα because Calypso lived in a cave.
But ἐν δώματα ναίει is unquestionably right.]

II. *From his MS. book of notes on Iliad* I—VII. 54.
Iliad III. 46 ἦ τοιόσδε ἐών. Amabant, credo, Hiatus; non
solum tolerabant. Dedit poeta ἦ τοιοῦτος ἐών. 212 (μύθους καὶ
μήδεα πᾶσιν ὕφαινον.) Casaubonus ad Theocritum c. IX. corrigit
ἔφαινον. Recte. ἔφαινον μύθους, in concione loquebantur. Sic Il.
σ. 295, Νήπιε, μηκέτι ταῦτα νοήματα φαῖν' ἐνὶ δήμῳ. 357. (διὰ μὲν
ἀσπίδος ἦλθε φαεινῆς ὄβριμον ἔγχος.) Saepe redit hic versiculus
qui si vere ab Homero est, Licentia nescio qua pronuntiabitur Δία
μὲν, ut Ἄρες, Ἄρες. Non enim tribrachys pro Dactylo hic ponitur

to correct Homer may be illustrated by a single example.
Priam, the aged king of Troy, is standing beside Helen
on the walls, and looking forth on the plain where
warriors are moving. He sees Odysseus passing along
the ranks of his followers, and asks Helen who that is.
'His arms lie on the earth that feedeth many: but he
himself, *like a leader of the flock* (κτίλος ὣς), moves along
the ranks of men; yea, I liken him to a young ram with
thick fleece, that passeth through a great flock of white
sheep.' Bentley, thinking that ὣς must be Ϝώς, had to
get rid of κτίλος somehow. 'Never yet,' says Bentley,
'have I seen a ram ordering the ranks of men. And
what tautology! He moves along, like a ram: and I
compare him to a ram!' And so he changes the ram into
a word meaning 'unarmed' (writing αὐτὰρ ψιλὸς ἐὼν
instead of αὐτὸς δὲ κτίλος ὣς), because the arms of Odysseus are said to be lying on the ground.

Bentley had done first-rate work on some authors who
would have rewarded him better than Homer,—better
than Horace or Manilius. It was his habit to enter
collations of manuscripts, or his own conjectures, in
the margins of his classical books. Some of these
books are at Cambridge. Many more are in the British
Museum. The *Gentleman's Magazine* for 1807 relates
how Kidd found 60 volumes, formerly Bentley's, at
the London bookseller Lackington's, to whom they had
been sold by Cumberland, and from whom they were at
once bought for the Museum by the Trustees. The complete list of the Bentley books in the British Museum

ad exprimendam Hastae celeritatem, non magis quam Molossus
pes trium longarum ad tarditatem exprimendam. Quid si legat
quis, Διαπρὸ μὲν, pede Proceleusmatico, ut 'capitibu' nutantes
pinus,' 'Parietibus textum caecis iter.'

comprises (omitting duplicates) 70 works. All, or nearly all, the manuscript notes which enrich these volumes have now been printed somewhere. The notes on Lucan, whom Bentley had intended to edit, were published by Cumberland in 1760. Among the most ingenious emendations are those on Nicander, the Greek physician of Colophon (circ. 150 B.C.), whose epic on venomous bites (*Theriaca*) Bentley had annotated at the request of Dr Mead. But the province of Greek and Roman literature in which these remains most strikingly illustrate Bentley's power is, on the whole, that of the comic drama.

He had sent Küster his remarks on two plays of Aristophanes,—the *Plutus* and *Clouds*. All the eleven comedies have his marginal notes in his copy of Froben's edition, now in the British Museum. These notes were first published by G. Burges in the *Classical Journal* XI.—XIV. For exact scholarship, knowledge, and brilliant felicity, they are wonderfully in advance of anything which had then been done for the poet. Porson is said to have felt the joy of a truly great scholar on finding that his own emendations of Aristophanes had been anticipated, in some seventy instances, by the predecessor whom he so highly revered. Bentley's emendations of Plautus are also very remarkable. They have been published, for the first time, by Mr E. A. Sonnenschein, in his edition of the *Captivi* (1880), from the Plautus in the British Museum which Bentley used; it is the second edition of Pareus (Frankfurt, 1623). All our twenty comedies have been touched more or less,—the number of Bentley's conjectures in each ranging from perhaps 20 to 150 or more.

As in Aristophanes, so in Plautus, Bentley sometimes

anticipated the best thoughts of later critics. Such coinci-
dences show how much he was in advance of his age.
Those conjectures of Bentley's which were afterwards
made independently by such men as Porson or Ritschl
were in most cases *certain ;* in Bentley's day, however,
they were as yet beyond the reach of everyone else.
Nor must we overlook his work on Lucretius. That
library of Isaac Voss which Bentley had vainly sought
to secure for Oxford carried with it to Leyden the two
most important MSS. of Lucretius,—one of the 9th
century (Munro's A), another of the 10th (B). Bentley
had to work without these. His notes,—first completely
published in the Glasgow edition of Wakefield (1813),—
fill only 22 octavo pages in the Oxford edition of 1818.
But their quality has been recognised by the highest
authority. Munro thinks that Bentley, if he had had the
Leyden MSS., 'might have anticipated what Lachmann
did by a century and a half.' Another labour also, in
another field, descended from Bentley to Lachmann: of
that we must now speak.

CHAPTER X.

DR JOHN MILL published in 1707 his edition of the Greek Testament, giving in foot-notes the various readings which he had collected by the labour of thirty years. To understand the impression which this work produced, it is necessary to recall the nature of its predecessors. The Greek text of the New Testament, as then generally read, was ultimately based on two sixteenth century editions ; that of Erasmus (Basel, 1516), which had been marked by much carelessness; and that due chiefly to Stunica, in the 'Complutensian' Polyglott (so called from *Complūtum*, or Alcalá de Henares) of Cardinal Ximenes, printed in 1514, and probably published in 1522. The folio edition printed by Robert Estienne at Paris in 1550 was founded on the text of Erasmus. The Elzevir editions, of which the first appeared in 1624, gave the text of Estienne as imperfectly revised by the reformer Beza. The second Elzevir edition (1633) declared this to be 'the text now received by all.' Hence it came to be known as the 'Received Text.'

The existence of various readings, though a well-known, was hardly a prominent fact. Some had been

given in the margin of the folio Estienne; Beza had
referred to others; more had been noticed by Walton in
the Greek Testament of his Polyglott (1657), and by
Bishop Fell in his small edition (1675). The sources of
textual evidence generally had been described and discussed with intelligence and candour by the French
scholar Simon (1689—95). But Mill's edition was the
first which impressed the public mind by marshalling a
great array of variants, roughly estimated at thirty
thousand. In his learnéd *Prolegomena* Mill often expressed opinions and preferences, but without supplying
any general clue to the labyrinth exhibited in his critical
notes.

The alarm felt in some quarters is strikingly shown
by Whitby's censure of Mill's edition (1710), in which he
goes so far as to affirm that the 'Received Text' can be
defended *in all places* where the sense is affected (*in iis
omnibus locis* lectionem textus defendi posse), and that
even in matters 'of lesser moment' it is 'most rarely'
invalidated. On the other hand, anti-Christian writers
did not fail to make capital of a circumstance which they
represented as impugning the tradition. Thus Anthony
Collins, in his 'Discourse of Free-Thinking,' specially
dwelt on Mill's 30,000 variants. In his published reply
to Collins (1713), Bentley pointed out that such variants
are perfectly compatible with the absence of any essential corruption, while he insisted on the value of critical
studies in their application to the Scriptures. Dr Hare,
in publicly thanking Bentley for this reply, urged him to
undertake an edition of the New Testament. Undoubtedly there was a wide-spread feeling that some systematic effort should be made towards disengaging a standard
text from the variations set forth by Mill.

Three years later (1716), Bentley received a visit from John James Wetstein, a Swiss, related to the Amsterdam publishers who had reprinted Bentley's Horace. Wetstein was then on leave of absence from his duties as a chaplain in the Dutch army. For years he had devoted himself with rare ardour to those critical studies of the New Testament which were afterwards embodied in his edition (1751—2). He had recently collated some Greek MSS. in the Library of Paris. ' On hearing this '—Wetstein writes—Bentley ' urged me to publish my collations, with his aid. I pleaded my youth, and the shortness of my leave of absence ; I asked him to undertake the work himself, and to use my collections. At length I moved the great critic to entertain a design of which he seemed to have had no thought before—that of editing the New Testament.'

It is assumed by Tregelles that Wetstein was mistaken in supposing that Bentley had not previously contemplated an edition. Bentley's *studies* on the New Testament dated, it is true, from his earliest manhood ; there are traces of them in his Letter to Mill (1691), no less than in his reply to Collins ; he had already collated the Alexandrine MS., and had been using the ' Codex Bezae ' (his ' Cantabrigiensis,' belonging to the University Library) since 1715. But it does not follow that Wetstein's statement is not accurate. The fact that Bentley was deeply studying a subject is never sufficient to prove that he meant to write upon it.

Now, at any rate, the plan was definitely formed, and Wetstein returned to Paris, in order to aid it by further collations. In April, 1716, Bentley announced his project in a remarkable letter to the Archbishop of Canterbury, Dr Wake. Monk hints, though he does not say,

that Bentley's object was 'to interest the public,' in view
of imminent law proceedings. I quite agree with Mr
A. A. Ellis, the editor of *Bentleii Critica Sacra*, that in
this case there is no real ground for such a suggestion.
Bentley's enthusiasm for the work was sincere, as his
correspondence with Wetstein abundantly shows; he did
not bring his scheme before the public till 1720; and his
object in addressing the Primate was no other than that
which he states, viz., to learn whether the project was
likely to be encouraged. After sketching his plan, he
observes to Dr Wake that it might be made for ever impossible by a fire in the Royal Library of Paris or London.
It is startling to read this foreboding, expressed in 1716.
Fifteen years later, a fire actually broke out at night in
the King's Library, then lodged at Abingdon House,
Westminster,—when the Cottonian Genesis was seriously
damaged. An eyewitness of the scene has described
Bentley hurrying out of the burning Library, in his
night-gown and his great wig, with the most precious of
his charges, the Alexandrine manuscript of the Greek
Bible, under his arm.

The Archbishop's reply to Bentley is not extant, but
appears to have been favourable. For the next four
years (1716—20) Bentley continued to gather materials.
Wetstein was not his only ally. David Casley, the
Deputy King's Librarian, worked for him in the libraries
of Oxford. More important still was the aid of John
Walker, a Fellow of Trinity College, who went to Paris
in 1719, and passed nearly a year there in collating
manuscripts. Walker was most kindly received by the
Benedictines of St Maur, with whom Bentley had already
been placed in communication by Wetstein. They provided him with a room in their monastery at St Germain

des Prés, procured collations from the Benedictines of Angers, and personally aided his work in their own library.

Walker returned from Paris in 1720. Bentley now published his 'Proposals for Printing,' in which he explains the principles of his edition. He observes that the printed texts of the New Testament, Greek and Latin, are based on comparatively recent manuscripts. His aim has been to recover from older Latin manuscripts the text of the Latin 'Vulgate' as formed by Jerome [about 383 A. D.], and to compare this with the oldest Greek manuscripts. Jerome's version was not only strictly literal, but aimed at representing the very order of the Greek words. Where it agrees with our oldest Greek manuscripts, there, Bentley argues, we may recognise the Greek text as received by the Church at the time of the Council of Nice (325 A. D.) 'and two centuries after.' This test will set aside about four-fifths of those 30,000 various readings which 'crowd the pages' of the editions. The text of the New Testament can be fixed 'to the smallest nicety.' As corroborative evidence, Bentley further proposes to use the Syriac, Coptic, Gothic, and Æthiopic versions (in which Walton's Polyglott would help him), and the citations by the Greek and Latin Fathers, within the first five centuries. Those centuries are to be the limit of the various readings which his foot-notes will exhibit. And he reassures the public mind on a point which might well occasion uneasiness. 'The author is very sensible, that in the Sacred Writings there's no place for conjectures or emendations.' He will not 'alter one letter in the text' without the authorities given in the notes, but will relegate conjectural criticism to the *Prolegomena*. The

work is to be 'a Charter, a Magna Charta, to the whole
Christian Church; to last when all the ancient MSS.
here quoted may be lost and extinguished.' As a
specimen of his edition, Bentley subjoined the last
chapter of Revelation, with notes supporting those
readings which he restores to the text, while the 'received'
readings, when displaced, are given in the margin.

The 'Proposals' had scarcely appeared when they
were anonymously attacked by Dr Conyers Middleton,
who was then in the midst of his feud with Bentley.
This was the year of the South-Sea scheme, and Dr
Middleton allowed himself to write of 'Bentley's Bubble.'
Bentley's reply—founded on the supposition that his
assailant was Colbatch—was still more deplorable. Middleton then printed, with his name, 'Some Further
Remarks,' criticising the 'Proposals' more in detail, and
on some points with force. Colbatch writes to Middleton:
'According to all that I can speak with or hear from,
you have laid Bentley flat upon his back.' Bentley
writes to Atterbury (now Bishop of Rochester): 'I scorn
to read the rascal's book; but if your Lordship will send
me any part which you think the strongest, I will undertake to answer it before night.'

Meanwhile the public subscription invited by the
'Proposals' already amounted, in 1721, to two thousand
pounds. Amid many distractions, Bentley was certainly continuing to digest his materials. At some
time before August, 1726, he received a most important accession to them. The 'Vatican' manuscript—which contains the Greek Testament in capital
letters as far as the middle of Hebrews ix.—was collated for Bentley by an Italian named Mico. Thomas
Bentley, the nephew, being at Rome in 1726, tested

Mico's work in three chapters, but did not, as has been supposed, make a complete independent collation. Subsequently the Vaticanus was again collated for Bentley, so far as concerned traces of hands other than 'the first,' by the Abbé Rulotta, whose services were procured by the Baron de Stosch,—then employed in Italy by the British Government to watch the Pretender. Rulotta's collation reached Bentley in July, 1729. Its accuracy, as compared with that of Angelo Mai, was recognised by Tischendorf, when he saw it at Trinity College in 1855. In that same summer of 1729 Bentley was making inquiries regarding a manuscript, in the Library of the University of Dublin, which contains the text of the three witnesses (1 John v. 7, 8): it is that which is known, from the name of the donor, as the Codex Montfortianus, and is not older than the fifteenth century. Considerable uneasiness appears to have been felt, after the issue of Bentley's 'Proposals,' at the prospect of his omitting that text, against which he had decided in his lost dissertation of 1717. It is unnecessary to remind readers that more recent criticism has finally rejected the words, for which there is no evidence in Latin before at least the latter part of the fifth century, and none in any other language before the fourteenth.

Here—in the summer of 1729—it has usually been said, as by Monk, that all vestige of the proposed edition ends. A slight but interesting trace, however, carries us three years further. From a marginal note in a copy of the quarto New Testament of Geneva (1620), preserved in the Wake collection at Christ Church, Oxford, it appears that John Walker was still making collations in 1732. These, it cannot be doubted, were auxiliary to Bentley's edition, for which the 'Proposals' designate Walker as 'overseer and corrector of the press.' Seven years more of working life remained to Bentley, before the paralytic seizure which overtook him in 1739. Why was his edition never completed and published? We need not pause on the curiously inadequate reason suggested by Wetstein—that Bentley resented the refusal of the Government to remit the duty on foreign paper which he desired to import. The dates alone refute that, for the incident occurred in 1721. Probably the answer is to be sought in a combination of two principal causes,—the worry of litigation which harassed him from 1729 to 1738 ; and a growing sense of complexity in the problem of the text, especially after he became better acquainted with the Vatican readings.

Bentley's materials were bequeathed by him to his nephew Richard, possibly in the hope that they might be edited and published. Nothing was done, however. Dr Richard Bentley returned the subscriptions, and at his death in 1786 bequeathed his uncle's collections to Trinity College, where they have since been preserved. Several volumes contain the collations made by Bentley himself or by his various assistants--including Mico's and Rulotta's collations of the Vaticanus. The point which Bentley's critical work had reached is best shown by a folio copy of the Greek and Latin Vulgate (Paris, 'apud Claudium Sonnium,' 1628). 'Having interleaved it'—he writes to Wetstein—'I have made my essay of restoring both text and version [*i.e.* both Greek and Latin]; and they agree and tally even to a miracle; but there will be (as near as I can guess) near 6000 variations, great and little, from the received Greek and Latin exemplars.' The notes on the interleaved pages are in Bentley's handwriting from the beginning to the end of the New Testament. He used this volume as a general register of results obtained by his collations,—the readings of the Vaticanus, which came to him after nearly all the rest, being added in paler ink. It is from this folio that Mr Ellis prints (besides excerpts) the whole of the Epistle to the Galatians, in his *Bentleii Critica Sacra* (1862) ; though it is to be observed that we cannot assume Bentley's final acceptance of the text, as there printed, except in the points on which he has expressly touched. The notes on Revelation xxii. stand in the folio *verbatim* as they were printed in the 'Proposals' of 1720. Speaking generally of the work exhibited by the folio, we may say that its leading characteristics are two ;—wealth of patristic citation, and laborious attention to the order of words. It may further be observed that there does not appear to be any trace of that confident temerity by which Bentley's treatment of the classics was so often marked. Had his edition been published, the promise made in the 'Proposals' would, in all probability, have been strictly kept. Conjectural criticisms would have been confined to the *Prolegomena*.

A question of great interest remains. What was the value of the principle on which Bentley founded his design, and how far has that principle been fruitful in later work ? Bentley's undertaking (as briefly defined in his letter to Dr Wake) was, 'to give an edition of the Greek Testament exactly as it was in the best exemplars at the time of the Council of Nice' (325 A.D.). He saw that, for this, our ultimate witnesses are the Greek manuscripts nearest in age to that time. But it might still be asked : How can we be sure that these oldest Greek manuscripts represent a text *generally*

received at the time when they were written? Bentley
replied : I compare them with the oldest received Latin
translation that I can find.   Such a received Latin version
must have represented a received Greek text.   Where it
confirms our oldest Greek manuscripts, there is the
strongest evidence that their text is not merely ancient,
but also is that text which the Church received at the
time when the Latin version was made.   The evidence
of the Fathers, and of ancient versions other than Latin,
may help to confirm the proof.

These, then, are the two features of Bentley's conception :—the appeal from recent documents to *antiquity*,—
viz. to the first five centuries; and the appeal to *Greek
and Latin consent*.

In the particular application of these ideas, Bentley
laboured under certain disadvantages which were either
almost or altogether inseparable from the time at which
he worked.   First, it was then scarcely possible that he
should adequately realise the history of the Greek text
previous to his chosen date, the Council of Nice.   The
Alexandrine manuscript, of the fifth century, containing
the whole of the New Testament in Greek capital
letters, had been presented to Charles I. by Cyril
Lucar, the Patriarch of Constantinople, in 1628.   This
was believed to be, as Bentley calls it, ' the oldest and
best in the world.'   It was regarded as the typical
ancient manuscript, not only by the earlier English
editors, Walton, Fell and Mill, but by Bengel in his
edition of 1734.   This view has since been modified by
data, some of which were not then available.   Not
less than two or three generations before the Council
of Nice (325 A.D.), according to the more recent investigations, two influential types of text had already

diverged from the apostolic original. These have been called the ' Western' and the 'Alexandrian.' Both are ' Pre-Syrian'—to use the convenient term adopted by Dr Westcott and Dr Hort—in distinction from the 'Syrian' Greek text formed at Antioch at some time between 250 and 350 A.D. The 'Syrian' text was eclectic, drawing on both the aberrant Pre-Syrian types, 'Western' and 'Alexandrian,' as well as on texts independent of those two aberrations. In a revised form, the Syrian text finally prevailed ; a result due partly to the subsequent contraction of Greek Christendom, partly to its centralisation at Constantinople, the ecclesiastical daughter of Antioch.

Four manuscripts of the 'uncial' class (written in capitals, as distinguished from 'cursive') stand out as the oldest Greek copies of the New Testament. Two belong probably to the middle of the fourth century. One of these is the Vatican manuscript, of which Bentley had no detailed knowledge at the time when he published his 'Proposals.' Its text is Pre-Syrian, and thus far unique, that in most parts it is free from both Western and Alexandrian corruptions. The other fourth-century manuscript is the Sinaitic, of which the New Testament portion first came into Tischendorf's hands in 1859. This also is Pre-Syrian, but with elements both Western and Alexandrian. The Codex Alexandrinus, which Bentley's age deemed the oldest and best, is fundamentally Syrian in the Gospels : in the other books it is still partially Syrian, though Pre-Syrian readings, Western and Alexandrian included, are proportionally more numerous. Thus it contains throughout at least one disturbing element which is absent from the Sinaitic, and at least three which in most of the books are absent

from the Vaticanus. The fourth of the oldest uncials is
one which Wetstein twice collated at Paris for Bentley,—
that known as the Codex Ephraemi, because some
writings attributed to Ephraem Syrus have been traced
over the New Testament. It is coeval with the Alexandrinus, belonging to the fifth century; and, while
partly Syrian, it also contains much derived from the
earlier texts. In addition to the general but erroneous
belief as to the unique value of the Alexandrine manuscript, a singular accident (noticed by Dr Hort) must
have greatly strengthened Bentley's belief in the decisive-
ness of the agreement between that document and the
Vulgate. Jerome, in preparing the Vulgate, appears to
have used a Greek manuscript which happened to have
many peculiar readings in common with the Alexandrinus,
and to have been partly derived from the same original.

The reader will now be able to imagine the effect
which must have been gradually wrought on Bentley's
mind, as he came to know the Vaticanus better. With
his rare tact and insight, he could hardly fail to perceive
that this was a document of first-rate importance, yet
one of which the evidence could not be satisfactorily
reconciled with the comparatively simple hypothesis
which he had based on the assumed primacy of the
Alexandrine. For his immediate purpose, it was of far
less importance that he was partly in error as to his
Latin standard. His view on that subject is connected
with a curious instance of his boldness in conjectural
criticism. Referring to 'interpretationes' or versions
of the Bible, Augustine once says, 'Let the Italian
(*Itala*) be preferred to the rest, since it combines greater
closeness with clearness' (*De Doctr. Chr.* II. 15). Bentley,
with a rashness which even he seldom exceeded, declared

that the 'Italian version is a mere dream:' *Itala*, in
Augustine, should be *illa*. Archbishop Potter's *usitata*,
viewed merely as an emendation, was far more intrinsically probable; but Cardinal Wiseman's arguments in
his letters (1832—3),—reinforced by Lachmann's illustrations,—have placed it beyond reasonable doubt that
Augustine really wrote *Itala*. As to his meaning, all
that is certain is that he intended to distinguish this
'Italian' text from the 'African' (*codices Afros*) which
he mentions elsewhere. Of a Latin version, or Latin
versions, prior to Jerome's—which was a recension, with
the aid of Greek MSS., not a new and original version—
Bentley could scarcely know anything. The documents
were first made accessible in Bianchini's *Evangeliarium
Quadruplex* (1749), and the Benedictine Sabatier's *Bibli-
orum Sacrorum Latinae Versiones Antiquae* (1751). It
must be remembered, however, that Bentley's aim was
to restore the text as received in the fourth century;
he did not profess to restore the text of an earlier age.

Bentley's edition would have given to the world the
readings of all the older Greek MSS. then known, and
an apparatus, still unequalled in its range of authorities,
for the text of the Latin Vulgate New Testament:
but it would have done more still. Whatever might
have been its defects, it would have represented the
earliest attempt to construct a text of the New Testament
directly from the most ancient documents, without reference to any printed edition. A century passed before
such an attempt was again made. Bentley's immediate
successors in this field did not work on his distinctive
lines. In 1726 Bengel's Greek Testament was almost
ready for the press, and he writes thus:—'What principally holds me back is the delay of Bentley's promised

edition...Bentley possesses invaluable advantages; but
he has prepossessions of his own which may prove
very detrimental to the Received Text:'—this 'received
text' being, in fact, the Syrian text in its mediæval
form. Bengel's text, published at Tübingen in 1734,
was not based on Bentley's principles, though the value
of these is incidentally recognised in his discussions.
Wetstein's edition of 1751—2 supplied fresh materials;
in criticism, however, he represents rather a reaction
from Bentley's view, for his tendency was to find
traces of corruption in any close agreement between the
ancient Greek MSS. and the ancient versions. Gries-
bach prepared the way for a properly critical text
by seeking an historical basis in the genealogy of the
documents.

But it was Lachmann, in his small edition of 1831,
who first gave a modified fulfilment to Bentley's design, by publishing a text irrespective of the printed
tradition, and based wholly on the ancient authorities.
Lachmann also applied Bentley's principle of Greek and
Latin consent. As Bentley had proposed to use the
Vulgate Latin, so Lachmann used what he deemed the
best MSS. of the Old Latin,—combined with some Latin
Fathers and with such Greek MSS. as were manifestly of
the same type. Lachmann compared this group of witnesses from the West with the other or 'Eastern' Greek
authorities; and, where they agreed, he laid stress on
that agreement as a security for the genuineness of readings. Bentley had intended to print the Greek text and
the Vulgate Latin side by side. Lachmann, in his larger
edition (1840—1852), so far executed this plan as to
print at the foot of the page a greatly improved Vulgate
text, based chiefly on the two oldest MSS. For Lach-

mann, however, the authority of the Vulgate was only accessory (' *Hieronymo* pro se *auctore non utimur* '), on account of the higher antiquity of the Old Latin. Those who taunted Lachmann with ' aping' Bentley ('simia Bentleii') misrepresented both. It is to Lachmann and to Tregelles that we primarily owe the revived knowledge and appreciation in this country of Bentley's labours on the New Testament, to which Tischendorf also accords recognition in his edition of 1859.

Bentley's place in the history of sacred criticism agrees with the general character of his work in other provinces. His ideas were in advance of his age, and also of the means at his disposal for executing them. He gave an initial impulse, of which the effect could not be destroyed by the limitation or defeat of his personal labours After a hundred years of comparative neglect, his conception reappeared as an element of acknowledged value in the methods of riper research. The edition of the New Testament published last year (1881) by Dr Westcott and Dr Hort represents a stage of criticism which necessarily lay beyond Bentley's horizon. Yet it is the maturest embodiment of principles which had in him their earliest exponent; and those very delays which closed over his great design may in part be regarded as attesting his growing perception of the rule on which the Cambridge Editors so justly lay stress ;—' Knowledge of documents should precede final judgement upon readings.'

CHAPTER XI.

As a writer of English, Bentley is represented by
the Dissertation on Phalaris, the Boyle Lectures, the
Remarks on a Discourse of Free-thinking, sermons, and
letters.   These fall mainly within the period from 1690
to 1730.   During the earlier half of Bentley's life the
canon of polite prose was Dryden or Temple; during
the latter half it was Addison.   Bentley's English is
stamped, as we shall see, with the mind of his age, but
has been very little influenced by any phase of its
manner.   His style is thoroughly individual; it is, in fact,
the man.   The most striking trait is the nervous, homely
English.   'Commend me to the man that with a thick
hide and solid forehead can stand bluff against plain
matter of fact.'   'If the very first Epistle, of nine lines
only, has taken me up four pages in scouring, what a
sweet piece of work should I have of it to cleanse all
the rest for them!'   'Alas, poor Sophist! 'twas ill luck
he took none of the money, to fee his advocates lustily;
for this is like to be a hard brush.'   The 'polite' writers
after the Restoration had discarded such English as vulgar;
and we have seen that Boyle's Oxford friends complained

of Bentley's 'descending to low and mean ways of speech.'
But, if we allow for the special influence of scriptural
language on the *Pilgrim's Progress*, Bentley drew from
the same well as John Bunyan, who died when Bentley
was sixteen.　Yet Bentley's simple English is racy in
a way peculiar to him.　It has the tone of a strong mind
which goes straight to the truth; it is pointed with the
sarcasm of one whose own knowledge is thorough and
exact, but who is accustomed to find imposture wrapped
up in fine or vague words, and takes an ironical delight
in using the very homeliest images and phrases which
accurately fit the matter in hand.　No one has excelled
Bentley in the power of making a pretentious fallacy
absurd by the mere force of translation into simple
terms; no writer of English has shown greater skill in
touching the hidden springs of its native humour.

Here Bentley is the exponent, in his own way, of
a spirit which animated the age of Addison and Pope,
—the assertion of clear common sense,—the desire,
as Mr Leslie Stephen says, 'to expel the mystery
which had served as a cloak for charlatans.'　Bentley's
English style reflects, however, another side on which he
was not in sympathy with the tendencies of contemporary literature.　A scholar of profound learning and
original vigour had things to say which could not
always be said with the sparkling ease of coffee-house
conversation.　Bentley's colloquialism is that of strenuous
argument, not that of polished small talk.　As an outward symbol of his separateness from the 'wits,' we
may observe his use of the Latin element in English.
The sermons of Jeremy Taylor, whose life closed soon
after Bentley's began, abound in portentous Latin words,
—*longanimity, recidivation, coadunation.*　Bentley has

nothing like these; yet the Boyle party, who charged his
style with vulgarity, charged it also with pedantry.

He answers this in the Dissertation on Phalaris. 'If
such a general censure had been always fastened upon
those that enrich our language from the Latin and
Greek stores, what a fine condition had our language
been in! 'Tis well known, it has scarce any words,
besides monosyllables, of its native growth; and were
all the rest imported and introduced by *pedants?*...
The words in my book, which he excepts against, are
*commentitious, repudiate, concede, aliene, vernacular, timid,
negoce, putid,* and *idiom;* every one of which were in
print, before I used them; and most of them, before I
was born.' We note in passing that all but three of this
list—*commentitious, putid, negoce*—have lived; and we
remember De Quincey's story about *negoce,*—that when
he was a boy at school (about the year 1798) the use of
this word by the master suggested to him that *otium cum
dignitate* might be rendered 'oce in combination with
dignity,'—which made him laugh aloud, and thereby for-
feit all 'oce' for three days. Then Bentley remarks that
the 'Examiner's' illustrious relative, Robert Boyle, had
used *ignore* and *recognosce*—'which nobody has yet
thought fit to follow him in.' It is curious to find De
Quincey saying, in 1830, that *ignore* is Irish, and obsolete
in England 'except in the use of grand juries;' and even
in 1857, it seems, some purists demurred to it. 'I would
rather use, not my own words only, but even these too'—
Bentley concludes—'than that single word of the Examiner's, *cotemporary,* which is a downright barbarism.
For the Latins never use *co* for *con,* except before a
vowel, as *coequal, coeternal;* but, before a consonant, they
either retain the N, as *contemporary, constitution;* or

melt it into another letter, as *collection, comprehension.*
So that the Examiner's *cotemporary* is a word of his
coposition, for which the learned world will *cogratulate*
him.'

Bentley's view as to the probable future of the English language appears from another place in the Dissertation. 'The great alterations it has undergone in the
two last centuries [1500—1700] are principally owing to
that vast stock of Latin words which we have trans-
planted into our own soil : which being now in a manner
exhausted, one may easily presage that it will not have
such changes in the two next centuries. Nay, it were
no difficult contrivance, if the public had any regard to
it, to make the English tongue immutable, unless here-
after some foreign nation shall invade and overrun us.'
This is in seeming contrast with Bentley's own description of language as an organism liable to continual
change, 'like the perspiring bodies of living creatures in
perpetual motion and alteration.' But the inconsistency,
I think, is only apparent. He refers to the English
vocabulary as a whole. By 'immutable' he does not
mean to exclude the action of time on details of form or
usage, but rather points to such a standard as the French
Academy sought to fix for the French language. Since
the end of the seventeenth century, the ordinary English
vocabulary has lost some foreign words, and acquired
others ; on the whole, the foreign element has probably
not gained ground. Here is a rough test. Mr Marsh
has estimated the percentage of English to non-English
words in several English classics. Swift's is about 70
(in one essay, only 68); Gibbon's, 70 ; Johnson's, 72 ;
Macaulay's, 75. Bentley's own average would, I think,
be nearly, if not quite, as high as Macaulay's, and for a

like reason ; his literary diction was comparatively close
to the living speech of educated men in his day. This,
indeed, is a marked feature of all Bentley's work, whatever the subject or form may be ; the author's personality
is so vividly present in it that it is less like writing than
speaking.

As in Shakspere, we meet with those faults of
grammar which people were apt to make in talking,
or which had even come to be thought idiomatic, through
the habit of the ear.   Bentley can say, 'neither of these
two improvements *are* registered,'—'*those* sort of requests,'
—'I 'll dispute with nobody about *nothing*' (meaning,
'about anything'),—'no goat had been there *neither.*'
This sympathy with living speech, and comparative
negligence of rigid syntax, may help us to see how
Bentley's genius was in accord with Greek, the voice
of life, rather than with Latin, the expression of law.
The scholarly trait of Bentley's style is not precise composition, but propriety in the use of words, whether of
English or of Latin growth.   Some of these Latinisms,
though etymologically right, seem odd now: 'an acuteness
familiar to him,' *i.e.* peculiarly his own : '*excision*' for
'utter destruction :' 'a plain and *punctual* testimony,'—
i.e. just to the point. Yet, on the whole, Bentley's
vocabulary contains a decidedly larger proportion of pure
English than was then usual in the higher literature.
No one is less pedantic.   At his best he is, in his own
way, matchless : at his worst, he is sometimes rough or
clumsy ; but he is never weak, and never anything else
than natural.   His style in hand-to-hand critical combat—
as in the Phalaris Dissertation—is that by which he is
best known.   I may here give a short specimen of a different manner, from a Sermon which he preached at

St James's in 1717. He is speaking on the words, 'none
of us liveth to himself' (Romans xiv. 7) :—

Without society and government, man would be found in
a worse condition than the very beasts of the field. That
divine ray of reason, which is his privilege above the brutes,
would only serve in that case to make him more sensible of
his wants, and more uneasy and melancholic under them.
Now, if society and mutual friendship be so essential and
necessary to the happiness of mankind, 'tis a clear consequence, that all such obligations as are necessary to maintain
society and friendship are incumbent on every man. No one,
therefore, that lives in society, and expects his share in the
benefits of it, can be said to live to himself.

No, he lives to his prince and his country ; he lives to his
parents and his family ; he lives to his friends and to all under
his trust ; he lives even to foreigners, under the mutual sanc-
tions and stipulations of alliance and commerce ; nay, he lives
to the whole race of mankind : whatsoever has the character of
man, and wears the same image of God that he does, is truly
his brother, and, on account of that natural consanguinity, has
a just claim to his kindness and benevolence.... The nearer
one can arrive to this universal charity, this benevolence to
all human race, the more he has of the divine character im-
printed on his soul; for *God is love*, says the apostle; he
delights in the happiness of all his creatures. To this public
principle we owe our thanks for the inventors of sciences and
arts; for the founders of kingdoms, and first institutors of
laws; for the heroes that hazard or abandon their own lives
for the dearer love of their country; for the statesmen that
generously sacrifice their private profit and ease to establish
the public peace and prosperity for ages to come.

And if nature's still voice be listened to, this is really not
only the noblest, but the pleasantest employment. For though
gratitude, and a due acknowledgment and return of kindness
received, is a desirable good, and implanted in our nature by
God himself, as a spur to mutual beneficence, yet, in the

J. B.   N

whole, 'tis certainly much more pleasant to love than to be beloved again. For the sweetness and felicity of life consists in duly exerting and employing those sociable passions of the soul, those natural inclinations to charity and compassion. And he that has given his mind a contrary turn and bias, that has made it the seat of selfishness and of unconcernment for all about him, has deprived himself of the greatest comfort and relish of life. Whilst he foolishly designs to live to himself alone, he loses that very thing which makes life itself desirable. So that, in a word, if we are created by our Maker to enjoy happiness and contentment in our being; if we are born for society, and friendship, and mutual assistance; if we are designed to live as men, and not as wild beasts of the desert; we must truly say, in the words of our text, that none of us *liveth to himself*.

It will be noticed that in the above extract there are no sentences of unwieldy length, no involved constructions, such as usually encumbered the more elaborate prose of the seventeenth century. Comparatively short sentences, and lucid structure, are general marks of Bentley's English; and here, again, he reflects the desire of his age for *clearness*. It has been said that the special work of the eighteenth century was to form prose style. Bentley has his peculiar place among its earlier masters.

Mention is due to the only English verses which he is known to have written after boyhood. When Johnson recited them, Adam Smith remarked that they were 'very well; very well.' 'Yes, they *are* very well, Sir,' said Johnson: 'but you may observe in what manner they are well. They are the forcible verses of a man of strong mind, but not accustomed to write verse; for there is some uncouthness in the expression.' A Trinity undergraduate had written a graceful imitation of Horace's Ode, *Angustam amice pauperiem pati* (III. ii.);

with which Bentley was so much pleased that he straight-
way composed a parody on it. The gist of the young
man's piece is that an exemplary student is secure of
applause and happiness; Bentley sings that he is pretty
sure to be attacked, and very likely to be shelved. The
choice of typical men is interesting; Newton, and the
geologist, John Woodward, for science; Selden, for erudition; for theological controversy, Whiston, whom the
University had expelled on account of his Arianism.
(The following is Monk's version : Boswell's differs in a
few points, mostly for the worse; but in v. 11 rightly
gives 'days and nights' for 'day and night.')

> Who strives to mount Parnassus' hill,
>   And thence poetic laurels bring,
> Must first acquire due force and skill,
>   Must fly with swan's or eagle's wing.
>
> Who Nature's treasures would explore,
>   Her mysteries and arcana know,
> Must high, as lofty NEWTON, soar,
>   Must stoop, as delving WOODWARD, low.
>
> Who studies ancient laws and rites,
>   Tongues, arts, and arms, all history,
> Must drudge, like SELDEN, days and nights,
>   And in the endless labour die.
>
> Who travels* in religious jarrs,   *? *travails*
>   Truth mix'd with error, shade with rays,
> Like WHISTON, wanting pyx and stars,
>   In ocean wide or sinks or strays.
>
> But grant our hero's hope, long toil
>   And comprehensive genius crown,
> All sciences, all arts his spoil,
>   Yet what reward, or what renown?

ENVY, innate in vulgar souls,
     Envy steps in and stops his rise;
Envy with poison'd tarnish fouls
     His lustre, and his worth decries.

He lives inglorious or in want,
     To college and old books confin'd;
Instead of learn'd, he's call'd pedànt;
     Dunces advanc'd, he's left behind:
Yet left content, a genuine stoic he,
     Great without patron, rich without South-sea.

The third line from the end is significant. He
had been mentioned for a bishopric once or twice, but
passed over. In 1709, when Chichester was vacant,
Baron Spanheim and the Earl of Pembroke (then Lord
High Admiral) had vainly used their interest for Bentley.
We have seen that in 1724—about two years after these
verses were written—he declined the see of Bristol.

Now we must consider Bentley's criticisms on
Paradise Lost. In 1725 an edition of that poem had
appeared with a Life of Milton by Elijah Fenton
(1683—1730), who helped Pope in translating the
Odyssey. Fenton incidentally suggested some corrections of words which, he thought, might have taken the
place of other words similar in sound. This seems to
have put Bentley on his mettle: at any rate, he is said
to have meditated notes in 1726. His edition of *Paradise Lost* appeared in 1732, and is said to have been immediately due to a wish expressed by Queen Caroline
'that the great critic should exercise his talents upon an
edition' of Milton, 'and thus gratify those readers who
could not enjoy his celebrated lucubrations on classical
writers.' It may safely be assumed, however, that the
royal lady did not contemplate any such work as our

Aristarchus produced. Probably she thought that the learning, especially classical learning, which enters so largely into Milton's epic would afford a good field for illustrative commentary to a classical scholar.

' 'Tis but common justice'—Bentley's preface begins —'to let the purchaser know what he is to expect in this new edition of *Paradise Lost.* Our celebrated Author, when he compos'd this poem, being obnoxious to the Government, poor, friendless, and, what is worst of all, blind with a *gutta serena,* could only dictate his verses to be writ by another.' The amanuensis made numerous mistakes in spelling and pointing; Bentley says that he has tacitly corrected these merely clerical errors. But there was a more serious offender than the amanuensis; namely, the *editor.* This person owes his existence to Bentley's vigorous imagination. 'The friend or acquaintance, whoever he was, to whom Milton committed his copy and the overseeing of the press, did so vilely execute that trust, that *Paradise* under his ignorance and audaciousness may be said to be *twice lost.*' This editor is responsible for many careless changes of word or phrase : for instance :

> on the secret top
> Of Horeb or of Sinai—

'secret' is this editor's blunder for 'sacred.' Bentley gives 48 examples of such culpable carelessness. But even that is not the worst. 'This suppos'd Friend (call'd in these Notes the Editor), knowing Milton's bad circumstances'—the evil days and evil tongues—profited by them to perpetrate a deliberate fraud of the most heartless kind. Having a turn for verse-writing, he actually interpolated many lines of his own : Bentley gives 66 of them as examples. They can always be

'detected by their own silliness and unfitness.' So much
for the half-educated amanuensis and the wholly depraved editor.   But Milton himself has made some
'slips and inadvertencies too:' there are 'some incon-
sistences [sic] in the system and plan of his poem, for
want of his revisal of the whole before its publication.'
Sixteen examples are then given. These are beyond
merely verbal emendation. They require 'a change both
of words and sense.' Bentley lays stress on the fact that
he merely suggests remedies for the errors due to Milton
himself, but does not 'obtrude' them : adding, 'it is
hoped, even these will not be found absurd, or disagreeing
from the Miltonian character;'—and he quotes from
Virgil : 'I, too, have written verses : me also the shep-
herds call a singer; but I will not lightly believe them.'
This is perhaps the only thing in the preface that
distinctly suggests senility : it afterwards gave rise to
this doggrel :—

> How could vile sycophants contrive
>   A lie so gross to raise,
> Which even Bentley can't believe,
>   Though spoke in his own praise?

The preface concludes with a glowing tribute to Milton's
great poem. Labouring under all this 'miserable de-
formity by the press,' it could still charm, like 'Terence's
beautiful Virgin, who in spite of neglect, sorrow, and
beggarly habit, did yet appear so very amiable.' There
is some real pathos in the following passage,—remarkable
as the only one (so far as I know) in Bentley's writings
where he alludes to the long troubles of his College
life as causes of *pain*, and not merely of interruption :—

But I wonder not so much at the poem itself, though
worthy of all wonder ; as that the author could so abstract his

thoughts from his own troubles, as to be able to make it; that confin'd in a narrow and to him a dark chamber, surrounded with cares and fears, he could spatiate at large through the compass of the whole universe, and through all heaven beyond it; could survey all periods of time, from before the creation to the consummation of all things. This theory [*i.e.* contemplation], no doubt, was a great solace to him in his affliction; but it shows in him a greater strength of spirit, that made him capable of such a solace. And it would almost seem to me to be peculiar to him; had not experience by others taught me, that there is that power in the human mind, supported with innocence and *conscia virtus;* that can make it quite shake off all outward uneasinesses, and involve itself secure and pleas'd in its own integrity and entertainment.

Bentley appears to have fully anticipated the strong prejudice which his recension of Milton would have to meet. Forty years ago, he says, 'it would have been prudence to have suppress'd' it, 'for fear of injuring one's rising fortune.' But now seventy years admonished him to pay his critical debts, regardless of worldly loss or gain. 'I made the Notes extempore, and put them to the press as soon as made; without any apprehension of growing leaner by censures or plumper by commendations.' So ends the preface.

Bentley's work on Milton is of a kind which can be fairly estimated by a few specimens, for its essential character is the same throughout. We need not dwell on those 'inconsistencies in the plan and system of the poem' which Bentley ascribes to Milton himself. Some of these are real, others vanish before a closer examination; but none of those which really exist can be removed without rewriting the passages affected. Bentley admits this; and to criticise his changes would be merely to compare

the respective merits of Milton and Bentley as poets.
Nor, again, need we concern ourselves with those alleged
faults of the amanuensis in spelling and pointing which
are tacitly corrected. The proper test of Bentley's work,
as a critical recension of *Paradise Lost*, is his treatment
of those blemishes which he imputes to the supposed
'editor.' These are of two kinds,—wilful interpolations
and inadvertent changes. An example of alleged interpolation is afforded by the following passage (*Par. Lost*
I. 338—355), where the fallen angels are assembling at
the summons of their leader :—

> As when the potent rod
> Of Amram's son, in Egypt's evil day,
> Waved round the coast, up-called a pitchy cloud
> Of locusts, warping on the eastern wind,
> That o'er the realm of impious Pharaoh hung
> Like Night, and darkened all the land of Nile;
> So numberless were those bad Angels seen
> Hovering on wing under the cope of Hell,
> 'Twixt upper, nether, and surrounding fires;
> Till, as a signal given, the uplifted spear
> Of their great Sultan waving to direct
> Their course, in even balance down they light
> On the firm brimstone, and fill all the plain :
> *A multitude like which the populous North*
> *Poured never from her frozen loins to pass*
> *Rhene or the Danaw, when her barbarous sons*
> *Came like a deluge on the South, and spread*
> *Beneath Gibraltar to the Libyan sands.*

The last five lines are rejected by Bentley as due to
the fraudulent editor.   Here is his note :—

After he [Milton] had compared the Devils for number
to the cloud of locusts that darken'd all Egypt, as before to
the leaves that cover the ground in autumn [v. 302, 'Thick

as autumnal leaves that strew the brooks In Vallombrosa'],
'tis both to clog and to lessen the thought, to mention here
the Northern Excursions, when all human race would be
too few. Besides the diction is faulty; *frozen loins* are im-
proper for *populousness;* Gibraltar is a new name, since those
inroads were made; and to spread from thence to the Libyan
sands, is to spread over the surface of the sea.

It would be idle to multiply instances of 'interpolation :' this is a fair average sample. I will now illustrate
the other class of ' editorial' misdeeds,—careless alterations.   Book VI. 509 :—

> up they turned
> Wide the celestial soil, and saw beneath
> The originals of Nature in their crude
> Conception ; sulphurous and nitrous foam
> *They found, they mingled, and, with subtle art*
> Concocted and adusted, they reduced
> To blackest grain, and into store conveyed.

Bentley annotates :—

It must be very subtle Art, even in Devils themselves,
to adust brimstone and saltpetre.   But then he mentions only
these two materials, which without *charcoal* can never make
gunpowder.

Here, then, is the last part of the passage, rescued
from the editor, and restored to Milton :—

> sulphurous and nitrous foam
> *They pound, they mingle, and with sooty chark*
> Concocted and adusted, they *reduce*
> To blackest grain, and into store *convey.*

Let us take next the last lines of the poem (XII.
641 f.) :—

> They, looking back, all the eastern side beheld
> Of Paradise, so late their happy seat,
> Waved over by that flaming brand; the gate
> With dreadful faces thronged and fiery arms.

Some natural tears they dropped, but wiped them soon;
The world was all before them, where to choose
Their place of rest, and Providence their guide.
They, hand in hand, with wandering steps and slow,
Through Eden took their solitary way.

Addison had remarked that the poem would close
better if the last two lines were absent. Bentley,—without
naming Addison, to whom he alludes as 'an ingenious and
celebrated writer,'—deprecates their omission. 'Without
them Adam and Eve would be left in the Territory and
Suburbane of Paradise, in the very view of the *dreadful*
faces.' At the same time, Bentley holds that the two lines
have been gravely corrupted by the editor. These are
his grounds:—

Milton 'tells us before, that Adam, upon hearing Michael's
predictions, was even surcharg'd with joy (XII. 372); was
replete with joy and wonder (468); was in doubt, whether he
should repent of, or rejoice in, his fall (475); was in great
peace of thought (558); and Eve herself was *not sad*, but full
of *consolation* (620). Why then does this distich dismiss our
first parents in anguish, and the reader in melancholy? And
how can the expression be justified, 'with wand'ring steps
and slow'? Why *wand'ring?* Erratic steps? Very im-
proper: when in the line before, they were guided by Providence. And why *slow?* when even Eve profess'd her readiness and alacrity for the journey (614):—'*But now lead on;*
In me is no delay.' And why 'their solitary way'? All
words to represent a sorrowful parting? when even their
former walks in Paradise were as solitary as their way now:
there being nobody besides them two, both here and there.
Shall I therefore, after so many prior presumptions, presume
at last to offer a distich, as close as may be to the author's
words, and entirely agreeable to his scheme?

Then hand in hand *with social steps their way*
Through Eden took, *with heav'nly comfort cheer'd.*'

The total number of emendations proposed by Bentley in *Paradise Lost* rather exceeds 800. Not a word of the received text is altered in his edition; but the parts believed to be corrupt are printed in italics, with the proposed remedy in the margin. Most of the new readings aim at stricter propriety in the use of language, better logic, or clearer syntax,—briefly, at 'correctness.' It is a significant fact that Pope liked many of them, and wrote '*pulchre*,' '*bene*,' '*recte*' opposite them in his copy of Bentley's edition,—in spite of that line in the *Dunciad* which describes our critic as having 'humbled Milton's strains.' But even where we concede that the new reading is what Milton ought to have given, we can nearly always feel morally certain that he did not give it. I have found only one instance which strikes me as an exception. It is in that passage of Book VI. (332) which describes Satan wounded by the sword of the archangel Michael :—

> from the gash
> A stream of nectarous humour issuing flowed
> Sanguine, such as celestial Spirits may bleed.

'Nectar' is the wine of the gods ; Homer has another name for the etherial juice which flows in their veins. Thus when Diomedes wounds the goddess Aphrodite :— '*The immortal blood of the goddess flowed forth, even ichor, such as flows in the veins of blessed gods*' (Iliad v. 389). For 'nectarous' Bentley proposed 'ichorous.' The form of Milton's verse—'such as celestial Spirits may bleed '—indicates that he was thinking of the Iliad, and no poet was less likely than Milton to confuse 'nectar' with 'ichor.' Bentley's correction, if not true, deserves to be so.

Johnson has characterised Bentley's hypothesis of the 'editor' in well-known terms :—' a supposition rash and groundless, if he thought it true; and vile and pernicious, if, as is said, he in private allowed it to be false.' Bentley cannot be impaled on the second horn of the dilemma.   No one who has read his preface, or, who understands the bent of his mind, will entertain the idea that he wished to impose on his readers by a fiction which he himself did not believe.   Monk has another explanation. 'The ideal agency of the reviser of *Paradise Lost* was only a device to take off the odium of perpetually condemning and altering the words of the great poet...   At the same time, *he was neither deceived himself*, nor intended to deceive others.'   But Monk has not observed that a passage in Bentley's preface expressly excludes this plausible view.   ' If any one' (says Bentley) 'fancy this *Persona* of an editor to be a mere Fantom, a Fiction, an Artifice to skreen Milton himself; let him consider these four and sole changes made in the second edition : I. 505, v. 638, xI. 485, 551....If the Editor durst insert his forgeries, even in the second edition, when the Poem and its Author had slowly grown to a vast reputation; what durst he not do in the first, under the poet's poverty, infamy, and an universal odium from the royal and triumphant party?'   The *Paradise Regained* and the *Samson Agonistes* are uncorrupted, Bentley adds, because Milton had then dismissed this editor.

There can be no doubt, I think, that Bentley's theory of the depraved editor was broached in perfect good faith.   True, he supposes this editor to have taken fewer liberties with Book xII.,—an assumption which suited his desire to publish before Parliament met.   But that is only an instance of a man bringing himself to believe

just what he wishes to believe. How he could believe
it, is another question. If he had consulted the Life of
Milton by the poet's nephew, Edward Phillips (1694), he
would have found some adverse testimony. *Paradise
Lost* was originally written down in small groups of some
ten to thirty verses by any hand that happened to be
near Milton at the time. But, when it was complete,
Phillips helped his uncle in carefully revising it, with
minute attention to those matters of spelling and pointing
in which the amanuensis might have failed. The first
edition (1667), so far from being 'miserably deformed
by the press,' was remarkably accurate. As Mr Masson
says, 'very great care must have been bestowed on
the revising of the proofs, either by Milton himself, or
by some competent person who had undertaken to see
the book through the press for him. It seems likely
that Milton himself caused page after page to be read
over slowly to him, and occasionally even the words to
be spelt out.' Bentley insists that the changes in the
second edition of 1674 were due to the editor. Phillips
says of this second edition :—'amended, enlarg'd, and
differently dispos'd as to the number of books' [xii.
instead of x., books vii. and x. being now divided] 'by
his own hand, that is by his own appointment.' But the
habit of mind which Bentley had formed by free conjectural criticism was such as to pass lightly over any such
difficulties, even if he had clearly realised them. He felt
confident in his own power of improving Milton's text;
and he was eager to exercise it. The fact of Milton's
blindness suggested a view of the text which he adopted;
not, assuredly, without believing it ; but with a belief
rendered more easy by his wish.

Bentley's *Paradise Lost* raises an obvious question.

We know that his emendations of Milton are nearly all bad. The general style of argument which he applies to Milton is the same which he applies to the classical authors. Are his emendations of these also bad? I should answer: Many of his critical emendations, especially Latin, are bad: but many of them are good in a way and in a degree for which *Paradise Lost* afforded no scope. It is a rule applicable to most of Bentley's corrections, that their merit varies inversely with the soundness of the text. Where the text seemed altogether hopeless, he was at his best; where it was corrupted, but not deeply, he was usually good, though often not convincing; where it was true, yet difficult, through some trick (faulty in itself, perhaps) of individual thought or style, he was apt to meddle overmuch. It was his forte to make rough places smooth; his foible, to make smooth places rough. If *Paradise Lost* had come to Bentley as a manuscript largely defaced by grave blunders and deeply-seated corruptions, his restoration of it would probably have deserved applause. The fact that his edition was regarded as a proof of dotage, shows how erroneously his contemporaries had conceived the qualities of his previous work. Bentley's mind was logical, positive, acute; wonderfully acute, where intellectual problems were not complicated with moral sympathies. Sending flashes of piercing insight over a wide and then dim field, he made discoveries; among other things, he found probable or certain answers to many verbal riddles. His 'faculty of divination' was to himself a special source of joy and pride: nor unnaturally, when we recall its most brilliant feats. But verbal emendation was only one phase of his work: and, just because it was with him a mental indulgence, almost a passion, we must guard against assuming that the

average success with which he applied it is the chief
criterion of his power.

The faults of Bentley's *Paradise Lost* are, in kind,
the faults of his Horace, but are more evident to an
English reader, and are worse in degree, since the
English text, unlike the Latin, affords no real ground
for suspicion. The intellectual acuteness which marks
the Horace is present also in the notes on *Paradise
Lost*, but seldom wins admiration, more often appears
ridiculous, because the English reader can usually see
that it is grotesquely misplaced. A great and characteristic merit of Bentley's classical work, its instructiveness
to students of a foreign language and literature, is necessarily absent here. And the book was got ready for the
press with extreme haste. Still, the editor of *Paradise
Lost* is not the Horatian editor gone mad. He is merely
the Horatian editor showing increased rashness in a still
more unfavourable field, where failure was at once so
gratuitous and so conspicuous as to look like self-caricature,
while there was no proper scope for the distinctive qualities
of his genius. As to poetical taste, we may at least make
some allowance for the standards of the 'correct' period;
let us think of Johnson's remarks on Milton's versifica-
tion, and remember that some of Bentley's improvements
on Milton were privately admired by Pope.

CHAPTER XII.

DOMESTIC LIFE. LAST YEARS.

At the age of thirty-eight, when explaining his delay to answer Charles Boyle, Bentley spoke of his own '*natural aversion to all quarrels and broils.*' This has often, perhaps, been read with a smile by those who thought of his later feuds. I believe that it was quite true. Bentley was a born student. He was not, by innate impulse, a writer, still less an aspirant to prizes of the kind for which men chiefly wrangle. But his self-confidence had been exalted by the number of instances in which he had been able to explode fallacies, or to detect errors which had escaped the greatest of previous scholars. He became a dogmatic believer in the truth of his own instinctive perceptions. At last, opposition to his decrees struck him as a proof of deficient capacity, or else of moral obliquity. This habit of mind insensibly extended itself from verbal criticism into other fields of judgment. He grew less and less fit to deal with men on a basis of equal rights, because he too often carried into official or social intercourse the temper formed in his library by intellectual despotism over the blunders of the absent or the dead. He was rather too apt to treat those who dif-

fered from him as if they were various readings that had
cropped up from 'scrub manuscripts,' or 'scoundrel
copies,' as he has it in his reply to Middleton. He liked
to efface such persons as he would expunge false concords,
or to correct them as he would remedy flagrant instances
of hiatus. This was what made him so specially unfit for
the peaceable administration of a College. It was hard
for him to be *primus inter pares*, first among peers, but
harder still to be *primus intra parietes*, to live within
the same walls with those peers. The frequent personal
association which the circumstances of his office involved
was precisely calculated to show him constantly on his
worst side. He would probably have made a better bishop,
—though not, perhaps, a very good one,—just because
his contact would have been less close and continual with
those over whom he was placed. Bentley had many of
the qualities of a beneficent ruler, but hardly of a consti-
tutional ruler. If he had been the sole heir of Peisistratus,
he would have bestowed the best gifts of paternal government on those Athenian blacksmiths to whom he compared
Joshua Barnes, and no swords would have been wreathed
with myrtle in honour of a tyrannicide.

This warm-hearted, imperious man, with affections
the stronger because they were not diffuse, was seen to
the greatest advantage in family life, either because his
monarchy was undisputed, or because, there, he could
reign without governing. His happy marriage brought him
four children,—Elizabeth and Joanna,—a son, William,
who died in earliest infancy,—and Richard, the youngest,
born in 1708, who grew to be an accomplished but
eccentric and rather aimless man ; enough of a dilettante
to win the good graces of Horace Walpole, and too little
of a dependent to keep them.

J. B.　　　　　　　　　　　　　　　O

It is pleasant to turn from the College feuds, and to
think that within its precincts there was at least such a
refuge from strife as the home in which these children
grew up. The habits of the Bentley household were
simple, and such as adapted themselves to the life of an
indefatigable student. Bentley usually breakfasted alone
in his library, and, at least in later years, was often not
visible till dinner. When the *Spectator* was coming out,
he took great delight in hearing the children read it aloud
to him, and—as Joanna told her son—'was so particularly
amused by the character of Sir Roger de Coverley, that he
took his literary decease most seriously to heart.' After
evening prayers at ten, the family retired, while Bentley,
'habited in his dressing-gown,' returned to his books. In
1708 his eyes suffered for a short time from reading at
night; but he kept up the habit long afterwards. The
celebrated 'Proposals for Printing' the Greek Testament
were drawn up by candle-light in a single evening.
Latterly, he had a few intimate friends at Cambridge,—
some five or six Fellows of the College, foremost among
whom was Richard Walker,—and three or four other
members of the University; just as in London his
intercourse was chiefly with a very small and select
group,—Newton, Dr Samuel Clarke, Dr Mead, and a few
more. 'His establishment,' says his grandson, 'was
respectable, and his table affluently and hospitably served.'
'Of his pecuniary affairs he took no account; he had
no use for money, and dismissed it entirely from his
thoughts.' Mrs Bentley managed everything. Can this
be the Bentley, it will be asked, who built the staircase
and the hen-house, and who practised extortion on the
Doctors of Divinity? The fact seems to be as Cumberland
puts it, that Bentley had no love of money for its own

sake. Many instances of his liberality are on record,
especially to poor students, or in literary matters. But
he had a strong feeling for the dignity of his station, and
a frank conviction that the College ought to honour itself
by seeing that his surroundings were appropriate ; and he
had also a Yorkshireman's share of the British dislike to
being cheated. Bentley's total income was, for his position,
but moderate, and his testamentary provision for his
family was sufficiently slender to exempt him from the
charge of penurious hoarding.

At one time Mrs Bentley and the children used to
make an annual journey to London, where the Master
of Trinity, as Royal Librarian, had official lodgings at
Cotton House. Then there was an occasional visit to the
Bernards in Huntingdonshire, or to Hampshire, after
Elizabeth, the eldest daughter, had married Mr Humphrey
Ridge of that county; and this was as much variety as
the wisdom of our ancestors desired. At Cambridge
Bentley took scarcely any exercise, except in pacing up
and down a terrace-walk by the river, which was made
when the Master's garden was laid out in 1717. We
hear, however, of his joining a fishing expedition to Over,
a place about six miles from Cambridge, though some
may doubt whether Bentley had the right temperament
for that pursuit. After middle age he was peculiarly
liable to severe colds,—a result of sedentary life,—
and was obliged to avoid draughts as much as possible.
From 1727 he ceased to preside in the College Hall
at festivals : and at about the same time he nominated
a deputy at the 'acts' in the Divinity School. In 1729 it
was complained that for many years he had discontinued
his attendance in the College Chapel. One incident has
good evidence. On an evening in 1724, just after his

degrees had been restored, he went to the Chapel ;
the door-lock of the Master's stall was so rusty that he
could not open it.   Here are some contemporary verses
preserved by Granger :—

> The virger tugs with fruitless pains ;
> The rust invincible remains.
> Who can describe his woful plight,
> Plac'd thus in view, in fullest light,
> A spectacle of mirth, expos'd
> To sneering friends and giggling foes ?
> Then first, as 'tis from fame receiv'd,
> (But fame can't always be believ'd,)
> A blush, the sign of new-born grace,
> Gleam'd through the horrors of his face.
> He held it shameful to retreat,
> And worse to take the lower seat.
> The virger soon, with nimble bound,
> At once vaults o'er the wooden mound,
> And gives the door a furious knock,
> Which forc'd the disobedient lock.

After 1734 he practically ceased to attend the meetings
of the Seniority : the last occasion on which he presided
was Nov. 8, 1737.   His inability or reluctance to leave
his house is shown in 1739 by a curious fact.   A Fellow
of a College had been convicted of atheistical views by a
private letter which another member of the same society
had picked up in the quadrangle,—and read.   The meeting
of the Vice-Chancellor's Court at which sentence was to
be passed was held at Trinity Lodge.   Dr Monk regards
this as 'a compliment to the father of the University,' but
there was also a simpler motive.   Only eight Heads of
Houses had attended in the Schools ; nine were required
for a verdict ; and, feeling the improbability of Bentley
coming to them, they went to Bentley.   On seeing the

accused—a puny person—the Master of Trinity observed,
—'What! is that the atheist? I expected to have seen
a man as big as Burrough the beadle!' Sentence was
passed—expulsion from the University.

It seems to have been soon after this, in 1739, that
Bentley had a paralytic stroke,—not a severe one,
however. He was thenceforth unable to move easily
without assistance, but we have his grandson's authority
for saying that Bentley 'to the last hour of his life possessed
his faculties firm and in their fullest vigour.' He called
himself—Markland says—'an old trunk, which, if you
let it alone, will last a long time; but if you jumble it
by moving, will soon fall to pieces.'

Joanna Bentley, the second daughter, was her father's
favourite child,—'Jug' was his pet-name for her,—and
she seems to have inherited much of his vivacity, with
rather more of his turn for humorous satire than was
at that period thought quite decorous in the gentle sex.
Her son seems inclined to apologise for it; and Dr
Monk, too, faintly hints his regret. At the age of eleven,
she was the 'Phœbe' of a Pastoral in the *Spectator*,—the
'Colin' being John Byrom, B. A., of Trinity; and, after
causing several members of the College to sigh, and a
few to sing, Joanna was married, in 1728, to Denison
Cumberland, of Trinity,—a grandson of the distinguished
Bishop of Peterborough. Their son, Richard Cumberland,
was a versatile author. Besides novels, comedies, and
an epic poem, he wrote the once popular *Observer*, and
Anecdotes of Spanish Painters. Goldsmith called him
'the Terence of England;' Walter Scott commented on
his tendency 'to reverse the natural and useful practice
of courtship, and to throw upon the softer sex the task of
wooing;' but Cumberland's name has no record more

pleasing than those *Memoirs* to which we chiefly owe our
knowledge of Bentley's old age.

It was early in 1740 that death parted the old man
from the companion who had shared so many years of
storm or sunshine beyond the doors, but always of happiness within them. Richard Cumberland was eight years
old when Mrs Bentley died. 'I have a perfect recollec-
tion of the person of my grandmother, and a full impression of her manners and habits, which though in some
degree tinctured with hereditary reserve and the primitive cast of character, were entirely free from the hy-
pocritical cant and affected sanctity of the Oliverians.'
(Her family, the Bernards, were related to the Cromwells.)
A most favourable impression is given by a letter—one
of those printed by Dr Luard at the end of Rud's *Diary*—
in which she discusses the prospect (in 1732) of the
College case being decided against Bentley. Her life
had been gentle, kindly, and unselfish : her last words,
which her daughter Joanna heard, were,—'It is all
bright, it is all glorious.' Dreary indeed must have been
Bentley's solitude now, but for his daughters. Elizabeth
had returned to her father's house after the death of her
husband, Mr Ridge; and henceforth Mrs Cumberland
was much at Trinity Lodge, with her two children,—
Richard, and a girl somewhat older. And now we get
the best possible testimony to the loveable elements in
Bentley's nature,—the testimony of children. 'He was
the unwearied patron and promoter of all our childish
sports....I have broken in upon him many a time' (says
Cumberland) 'in his hours of study, when he would put
his book aside, ring his hand-bell for his servant, and be
led to his shelves to take down a picture-book for my
amusement. I do not say that his good-nature always

gained its object, as the pictures which his books generally supplied me with, were anatomical drawings of
dissected bodies,...but he had nothing better to produce.'
'Once, and only once, I recollect his giving me a gentle
rebuke for making a most outrageous noise in the room
over his library, and disturbing him in his studies ; I had
no apprehension of anger from him, and confidently
answered that I could not help it, as I had been at
battledore and shuttlecock with Master Gooch, the
Bishop of Ely's son.' (This was the Dr Gooch who,
as Vice-Chancellor, had suspended Bentley's degrees.)
'And I have been at this sport with his father,' he replied ; 'but thine has been the more amusing game ; so
there's no harm done.' The boy's holidays from his
school at Bury St Edmund's were now often spent at
Trinity Lodge, and in the bright memories which they
left with him his grandfather was the central figure. 'I
was admitted to dine at his table, had my seat next to
his chair, served him in many little offices.' Bentley
saw what pleasure these gave the boy, and invented
occasions to employ him.

Bentley's 'ordinary style of conversation was naturally lofty'—his grandson says. He also used *thou* and
thee more than was usually considered polite, and this gave
his talk a somewhat dictatorial tone. 'But the native
candour and inherent tenderness of his heart could not
long be veiled from observation, for his feelings and
affections were at once too impulsive to be long repressed,
and he too careless of concealment to attempt at quali-
fying them.' Instances of his good-nature are quoted
which are highly characteristic in other ways too. At
that time the Master and Seniors examined candidates
for Fellowships orally as well as on paper. If Bentley

saw that a candidate was nervous, he 'was never known
to press him,' says Cumberland; rather he 'would take
all the pains of expounding on himself'—and credit the
embarrassed youth with the answer. Once a burglar
who had stolen some of Bentley's plate was caught 'with
the very articles upon him,' and 'Commissary Greaves'
was for sending him to gaol. Bentley interposed. 'Why
tell the man he is a thief? He knows that well enough,
without thy information, Greaves.—Hark ye, fellow,
thou see'st the trade which thou hast taken up is an
unprofitable trade; therefore get thee gone, lay aside an
occupation by which thou can'st gain nothing but a
halter, and follow that by which thou may'st earn an
honest livelihood.' Everybody remonstrated, but the
burglar was set at large. This was a thoroughly Bent-
leian way of showing how the quality of mercy can bless
him that gives and him that takes. He never bestowed
a thought on the principle; he was preoccupied by his
own acute and confident perception that *this* man would
not steal again; and he disposed of Commissary Greaves
as if he had been a mere gloss, a redundant phrase due
to interpolation.

Next to the Vice-Master, Dr Walker—to whom in
1739 the duties of Master were virtually transferred—
Bentley's most frequent visitors were a few scholars,—
such as Jeremiah Markland, an ingenious critic, with a
real feeling for language,—Walter Taylor, the Regius
Professor of Greek,—John Taylor, the well-known
editor of Lysias and Demosthenes; and the two nephews,
Thomas and Richard Bentley. At seventy, he learned
to smoke; and he is believed to have liked port, but to
have said of claret that 'it would be port if it could.'
He would sometimes speak of his early labours and aims,

but the literary subject uppermost in his mind seems to have been his Homer. One evening, when Richard Cumberland was at the Lodge in his holidays, his schoolmaster, Arthur Kinsman, called with Dr Walker. Kinsman 'began to open his school-books upon Bentley, and had drawn him into Homer; Greek now rolled in torrents from the lips of Bentley,...in a strain delectable, indeed, to the ear, but not very edifying to poor little me and the ladies.'

In March, 1742—about four months before Bentley's death—the fourth book of the *Dunciad* came out, with Pope's highly-wrought but curiously empty satire on the greatest scholar then living in England or in Europe. Bentley heads an academic throng who offer homage at the throne of Dulness:—

> Before them march'd that awful Aristarch,
> Plow'd was his front with many a deep remark:
> His hat, which never vail'd to human pride,
> Walker with rev'rence took, and laid aside.

Then Bentley introduces himself to the goddess as

> Thy mighty scholiast, whose unwearied pains
> Made Horace dull, and humbled Milton's strains.

The final touch—'Walker, our hat!—nor more he deign'd to say'—was taken from a story current then. Philip Miller, the botanist, had called on Bentley at Trinity Lodge, and after dinner plied him with classical questions until Bentley, having exhausted such mild hints as 'drink your wine, Sir!', exclaimed, 'Walker! my hat'—and left the room. Cumberland remembers the large, broad-brimmed hat hanging on a peg at the back of Bentley's arm-chair, who sometimes wore it in his study to shade his eyes; and after his death it could

be seen in the College-rooms of the friend with whose
name Pope has linked it.

Pope had opened fire on Bentley long before this.
The first edition of the *Dunciad* (1728) had the line—
'*Bentley* his mouth with classic flatt'ry opes'—but in the
edition of 1729 'Bentley' was changed to *Welsted:* and
when—after Bentley's death—his name was once more
placed there, it was explained as referring to *Thomas* Bentley, the nephew. Then in the 'Epistle to Arbuthnot'
(1735) Pope coupled Bentley with the Shaksperian critic
Theobald,—'Tibbalds' rhyming to 'ribalds;' and in the
Epistle imitating that of Horace to Augustus (1737), after
criticising Milton, adds :—

> Not that I'd lop the beauties from his book,
> Like slashing Bentley with his desp'rate hook.

Some indignant protest from Thomas Bentley seems
to have roused Pope's ire to the more elaborate attack in
the fourth book of the *Dunciad*. Why did Pope dislike
Bentley ? 'I talked against his Homer'—this was Bentley's own account of it—'and the portentous cub never
forgives.' It is more likely that some remarks had been
repeated to Pope, than that Bentley should have said to
the poet at Bishop Atterbury's table, 'A pretty poem, Mr
Pope, but you must not call it Homer.' This was gossip
dramatising the cause of the grudge. Then Pope's
friendship with Atterbury and Swift would lead him to
take the Boyle view of the Phalaris affair. And Warburton, Pope's chief ally of the *Dunciad* period, felt towards Bentley that peculiar form of jealous antipathy
with which an inaccurate writer on scholarly subjects
will sometimes regard scholars. After Bentley's death,
Warburton spoke of him as 'a truly great and injured
man,' &c.; before it, he invariably, though timidly, dis-

paraged him. Swift never assailed Bentley after the *Tale of a Tub*. But Arbuthnot, another member of the Scriblerus Club, parodied Bentley's Horace and Phaedrus in the *Miscellanies* of 1727 ; and published a supplement to *Gulliver's Travels*, describing 'The State of Learning in the Empire of Lilliput.' 'Bullum is a tall raw-boned man, I believe near six inches and a half high ; from his infancy he applied himself with great industry to the old Blefuscudian language, in which he made such a progress that he almost forgot his native Lilliputian '—an unlucky stroke, seeing that Bentley's command of English was one of his marked gifts. This, however, is characteristic of all the satire directed against Bentley by the literary men who allowed a criticism of taste, but treated a criticism of texts as soulless pedantry. There is plenty of banter, but not one point. And the cause is plain,—they understood nothing of Bentley's work. Take Pope's extended satire in the fourth *Dunciad*. It is merely a series of variations, as brilliant and as thin as Thalberg's setting of ' Home, sweet home,' on the simple theme, ' dull Bentley.' A small satellite of Pope, one David Mallet, wrote a ' Poem on Verbal Criticism,' in which he greets Bentley as ' great eldest-born of Dulness '! Mallet deserves to be remembered with Garth.

In June, 1742, having completed eighty years and some months, Bentley was still able to examine for the Craven University Scholarships,—when Christopher Smart was one of the successful competitors. A few weeks later the end came. His grandson tells it thus. 'He was seized with a complaint' (pleuritic fever, it was said) 'that in his opinion seemed to indicate a necessity of immediate bleeding ; Dr Heberden, then a young physician practising in Cambridge, was of a contrary opinion,

and the patient acquiesced.' Bentley died on July 14,
1742. Dr Wallis, of Stamford—an old friend and adviser who was summoned, but arrived too late—said that
the measure suggested by the sufferer was that which he
himself would have taken.

Bentley was buried in the chapel of Trinity College,
on the north side of the communion-rails. The Latin
oration then customary was pronounced by Philip Yonge,
afterwards Public Orator, and Bishop of Norwich. The
day of Bentley's funeral was that on which George Baker
left Eton for King's College,—the eminent physician to
whom it was partly due that Cambridge became the University of Porson. The small square stone in the pave-
ment of the College Chapel bears these words only :—

H. S. E.

RICHARDUS BENTLEY S. T. P. R.

Obiit xiv. Jul. 1742.

Ætatis 80.

[Sanctae
Theologiae
Professor
Regius.]

The words *Magister Collegii* would naturally have
been added to the second line : but in the view of those
Fellows who acknowledged the judgment of April, 1738,
the Mastership had since then been vacant. In the hall
of the College, where many celebrated names are com-
memorated by the portraits on the walls, places of honour
are assigned to Bacon, Barrow, Newton, and Bentley.
The features of the great scholar speak with singular
force from the canvas of Thornhill, who painted him
in his forty-eighth year, the very year in which his
struggle with the College began. That picture, Bentley's
own bequest, is in the Master's Lodge. The pose of the
head is haughty, almost defiant; the eyes, which are
large, prominent, and full of bold vivacity, have a light

in them as if Bentley were looking straight at an impos-
tor whom he had detected, but who still amused him;
the nose, strong and slightly tip-tilted, is moulded as if
nature had wished to show what a nose can do for the
combined expression of scorn and sagacity; and the
general effect of the countenance, at a first glance, is one
which suggests power—frank, self-assured, sarcastic, and,
I fear we must add, insolent: yet, standing a little
longer before the picture, we become aware of an essential
kindness in those eyes of which the gaze is so direct and
intrepid; we read in the whole face a certain keen vera-
city; and the sense grows,—this was a man who could
hit hard, but who would not strike a foul blow, and whose
ruling instinct, whether always a sure guide or not, was
to pierce through falsities to truth.

CHAPTER XIII.

It will not be the object of these concluding pages to
weigh Bentley's merits against those of any individual
scholar in past or present times. The attempt, in such a
case, to construct an order of merit amuses the competitive
instinct of mankind, and may be an interesting exercise
of private judgment, but presupposes a common measure
for claims which are often, by their nature, incommen-
surable. A more useful task is to consider the nature of
Bentley's place in that development of scholarship which
extends from the fifteenth century to our own day. Caution may be needed to avoid drawing lines of a delusive
sharpness between periods of which the characteristics
rather melt into each other. The fact remains, however,
that general tendencies were successively prevalent in
a course which can be traced. And Bentley stands in
a well-marked relation both to those who preceded and to
those who followed him.

At his birth in 1662 rather more than two centuries
had elapsed since the beginning of the movement which was
to restore ancient literature to the modern world. During
the earlier of these two centuries—from about 1450 to

1550—the chief seat of the revival had been Italy, which thus retained by a new title that intellectual primacy of Europe which had seemed on the point of passing from the lands of the south. Latin literature engrossed the early Italian scholars, who regarded themselves as literary heirs of Rome, restored to their rights after ages of dispossession. The beauty of classical form came as a surprise and a delight to these children of the middle age; they admired and enjoyed; they could not criticise. The more rhetorical parts of silver Latinity pleased them best; a preference natural to the Italian genius. And meanwhile Greek studies had remained in the background. The purest and most perfect examples of form,—those which Greek literature affords,—were not present to the mind of the earlier Renaissance. Transalpine students resorted to Italy as for initiation into sacred mysteries. The highest eminence in classical scholarship was regarded as a birthright of Italians. The small circle of immortals which included Poggio and Politian admitted only one foreigner, Erasmus, whose cosmopolitan tone gave no wound to the national susceptibility of Italians, and whose conception, though larger than theirs, rested on the same basis. That basis was the *imitatio veterum*, the literary reproduction of ancient form. Erasmus was nearer than any of his predecessors or contemporaries to the idea of a critical philology. His natural gifts for it are sufficiently manifest. But his want of critical method, and of the sense which requires it, appears in his edition of the Greek Testament.

In the second half of the sixteenth century a new period is opened by a Frenchman of Italian origin, Joseph Scaliger. Hitherto scholarship had been busy

with the form of classical literature. The new effort is
to comprehend the matter. By his Latin compositions
and translations Scaliger is connected with the Italian
age of Latin stylists. But his most serious and characteristic work was the endeavour to frame a critical
chronology of the ancient world. He was peculiarly
well-fitted to effect a transition from the old to the new
aim, because his industry could not be reproached with
dulness. 'People had thought that æsthetic pleasure
could be purchased only at the cost of criticism,' says
Bernays; 'now they saw the critical workshop itself lit
up with the glow of artistic inspiration.' A different
praise belongs to Scaliger's great and indefatigable contemporary, Isaac Casaubon. His groans over Athenaeus,
which sometimes reverberate in the brilliant and faithful
pages of Mr Pattison, appear to warrant Casaubon's comparison of his toils to the labours of penal servitude
('*catenati in ergastulo labores*'). Bernhardy defines the
merit of Casaubon as that of having been the first to
popularise a connected knowledge of ancient life and
manners. Two things had now been done. The charm
of Latin style had been appreciated. The contents of
ancient literature, both Latin and Greek, had been surveyed, and partly registered.

Bentley approached ancient literature on the side
which had been chiefly cultivated in the age nearest to
his own. When we first find him at work, under
Stillingfleet's roof, or in the libraries of Oxford, he is
evidently less occupied with the form than with the
matter. He reads extensively, making indexes for his
own use; he seeks to possess the contents of the classical
authors, whether already printed or accessible only in
manuscript. An incident told by Cumberland is sug-

gestive. Bentley was talking one day with his favourite daughter, when she hinted a regret that he had
devoted so much of his time to criticism, rather than to
original composition. He acknowledged the justice of the
remark. 'But the wit and genius of those old heathens,'
he said, 'beguiled me: and as I despaired of raising
myself up to their standard upon fair ground, I thought
the only chance I had of looking over their heads was to
get upon their shoulders.' These are the words of a man
who had turned to ancient literature in the spirit of
Scaliger rather than in that of the Italian Latinists.

But in the Letter to Mill,—when Bentley was only
twenty-eight,—we perceive that his wide reading had already made him alive to the necessity of a work which no
previous scholar had thoroughly or successfully undertaken.
This work was the purification of the classical texts.
They were still deformed by a mass of errors which could
not even be detected without the aid of accurate
knowledge, grammatical and metrical. The great scholars
before Bentley, with all their admirable merits, had in
this respect resembled aeronauts, gazing down on a
beautiful and varied country, in which, however, the
pedestrian is liable to be stopped by broken bridges or
quaking swamps. These difficulties of the ground, to
which Bentley's patient march had brought him, engaged
his *first* care. No care could hope to be successful—this
he saw clearly—unless armed with the resources which
previous scholarship had provided. The critic of a text
should command the stylist's tact in language, and also
the knowledge of the commentator. In the Latin preface
to his edition of Horace, Bentley explains that his work
is to be textual, not illustrative ; and then proceeds :—

All honour to the learned men who have expatiated in the
field of commentary. They have done a most valuable work,

J. B.   P

which would now have to be done from the beginning, if they
had not been beforehand ; a work without which my reader
cannot hope to pass the threshold of these present labours.
That wide reading and erudition, that knowledge of all Greek
and Latin antiquity, in which the commentaries have their very
essence, are merely subordinate aids to textual criticism. A
man should have all that at his fingers' ends, before he can
venture, without insane rashness, to pass criticism on any
ancient author. But, besides this, there is need of the keenest
judgment, of sagacity and quickness, of a certain divining tact
and inspiration (*divinandi quadam peritia et* μαντικῇ), as was
said of Aristarchus,—a faculty which can be acquired by no
constancy of toil or length of life, but comes solely by the gift
of nature and the happy star.

Let it be noted that Bentley's view is relative to his
own day. It is because such men as Casaubon have gone
before that he can thus define his own purpose. Learning,
inspired by insight, is now to be directed to the attainment
of textual accuracy. Bentley's distinction is not so much
the degree of his insight,—rare as this was,—but rather
his method of applying it. It might be said :—Bentley
turned the course of scholarship aside from grander
objects, philosophical, historical, literary,—and forced it
into a narrow verbal groove. If Bentley's criticism had
been verbal only—which it was not—such an objection
would still be unjust. We in these days are accustomed
to Greek and Latin texts which, though they may be still
more or less unsound, are seldom so unsound as largely to
obscure the author's meaning, or seriously to mar our
enjoyment of his work as a work of art. But for this
state of things we have mainly to thank the impulse given
by Bentley.

In Bentley's time very many Latin authors, and
nearly all Greek authors, were known only through texts
teeming with every fault that could spring from a

scribe's ignorance of grammar, metre, and sense. Suppose a piece of very bad English handwriting, full of erasures and corrections, sent to be printed at a foreign press. The foreign printer's first proof would be likely to contain some flagrant errors which a very slight acquaintance with our language would suffice to amend, and also many other errors which an Englishman could correct with more or less confidence, but in which a foreign corrector of the press would not even perceive anything amiss. In 1700 most of the classical texts, especially Greek, were very much what such a proof-sheet would be if only those flagrant errors had been removed which a very imperfect knowledge of English would reveal. Relatively to his contemporaries, Bentley might be compared with the Englishman of our supposed case, and his predecessors with the foreign correctors of the press.

Space fails for examples, but I may give one. An epigram of Callimachus begins thus ;—

τὴν ἁλίην Εὔδημος, ἐφ᾽ ἧς ἅλα λιτὸν ἐπελθὼν
χειμῶνας μεγάλους ἐξέφυγεν δανέων,
θῆκε θεοῖς Σαμόθραξι.

This had been taken to mean :—'*Eudemus dedicated to the Samothracian gods that ship on which, after crossing a smooth sea, he escaped from great storms* [reading Δαναῶν] *of the Danai ;*'—*i.e.* such storms as Æneas and his companions suffered; or perhaps, storms off the coast of the Troad. Bentley changed one letter only (λ to σ, giving ἐπέσθων), and showed the true meaning. '*Eudemus dedicated to the Samothracian gods that salt-cellar from which he ate frugal salt until he had escaped from the troublous waves of usury.*' Eudemus was not an adventurous mariner, but an impecunious person who had literally adopted the advice of the Greek sage,—'Borrow from thyself by reducing thy diet,'—and had gradually extricated himself from debt by living on bread and salt.

The pleader for large views of antiquity, who is inclined to depreciate the humbler tasks of verbal criticism, will allow that the frequency of such misapprehensions was calculated to confuse. It was not always, indeed, that Bentley drew the veil aside with so light a touch; but he has a reason to give. 'I would have you remember, it is immeasurably more difficult to make emendations at this day (in 1711) than it was in former years. Those points which a mere collation of the manuscripts flashed or forced upon the mind have generally been seized and appropriated; and there is hardly anything left, save what is to be extracted, by insight alone, from the essence of the thought and the temper of the style. Hence, in my recension of Horace, I give more things on conjecture than through the help of manuscripts; and unless I am wholly deceived, conjecture has usually been the safer guide. Where readings vary, the very repute of the manuscript often misleads, and provokes the desire of change. But if a man is tempted to propose conjectures against the witness of all the manuscripts, Fear and Shame pluck him by the ear; his sole guides are reason,—the light from the author's thoughts, and their constraining power. Suppose that one or two manuscripts furnish a reading which others discountenance. It is in vain that you demand belief for your one or two witnesses against a multitude, unless you bring as many arguments as would almost suffice to prove the point of themselves, without any manuscript testimony at all. Shake off, then, the exclusive reverence for scribes. Dare to have a mind of your own. Gauge each reading by the mould of the writer's expression and the stamp of his style; then, and not sooner, pronounce your verdict.'

No school of textual criticism, however conservative, has denied that conjecture is sometimes our sole resource. Bentley differs from the principles of more recent criticism chiefly in recognising less distinctly that conjecture should be the *last* resource. Great as was his tact in the use of manuscripts, he had, as a rule, too little of that respect for diplomatic evidence which appears, for instance, in Ritschl's remark that almost any manuscript will sometimes, however rarely, deserve more belief than we can give even to a conjecture which is intrinsically probable. The contrast, here, between Bentley's procedure and that of Casaubon,—whose caution is often more in the spirit of modern textual science,—may be illustrated by one example. Some verses of the poet Ion stood thus in the texts of the geographer Strabo :—

Εὐβοΐδα μὲν γῆν λεπτὸς Εὐρίπου κλύδων
Βοιωτίας ἐχώρισ᾽ ἀκτῆς, ἐκτέμνων
πρὸς Κρῆτα πορθμόν.

When Casaubon had made the necessary change ἐκτεμών, he held his hand. 'I can point out,' said Casaubon, 'that this place is corrupt : amend it I cannot, *without the help of manuscripts.*' Not so Bentley : he confidently gives us, ἀκτὴν ἐκτεμὼν | προβλῆτα πορθμῷ. Now, if Casaubon was ineffectual, Bentley was precipitate. Nothing, surely, was needed but to shift Βοιωτίας from the beginning to the end of its verse. If we suppose that the words πρὸς Κρῆτα πορθμόν belonged to what precedes, and not (as is quite possible) to something now lost which followed, then we get a clear sense, expressed in a thoroughly classical form. 'The narrow waters of the Euripus have parted Euboea from the Boeotian shore, so shaping it (ἐκτεμών), that it looks toward the Cretan sea :' *i.e.* the island of Euboea runs out in a S. E. S. direction. Ancient writers often denote *aspect* by naming a region, though distant and invisible, towards which a land looks. Thus Herodotus describes a part of the north Sicilian coast as that which 'looks towards Tyrrhenia' (πρὸς Τυρσηνίην τετραμμένη). Milton imitates this device:

> Where the great vision of the guarded Mount
> Looks towards Namancos and Bayona's hold.

I never understood how Milton came to write those lines till I thought of seeking a clue in Camden (of whom there is another trace in *Lycidas*);—and he gave it. Speaking of the Cornish coast adjacent to St Michael's Mount, Camden remarks, 'there is no other place in this island that looks towards Spain.' This fact was present to Milton's mind, and he wished to work it in; then he consulted Mercator's Atlas, where he found the town of Namancos marked near Cape Finisterre, and the Castle of Bayona also prominent; these gave him his ornate periphrasis for 'Spain.'

Though Bentley had little poetical taste, it was in poetry that he exercised his faculty of emendation, not only with most zest, but with most success. The reason is simple. Metre enabled Bentley to show a knowledge in which no predecessor had equalled him; it also supplied a framework which limited his rashness. In prose, his temerity was sometimes wanton. We have seen (chapter x.) how his *illa* would have swept *Itala* from the text of Augustine. One other instance may be given. Seneca compares a man who cannot keep his temper to one who cannot control his limbs. 'Aegros scimus nervos esse, cum invitis nobis moventur. Senex aut infirmi corporis est, qui, cum ambulare vult, *currit*.' 'We know that something is wrong with our nerves, when they act against our will. It is only an old man, or an invalid, who, when he means to walk, *runs*.' By '*currit*,' Seneca describes a well-known symptom of degeneration in the nervous system, which modern medical science terms 'festination.' 'Now,' says Bentley, 'I do not see how this feeble person can show such agility. Clearly *currit* should be *corruit*. He tries to walk—and *tumbles down*.' Bentley did not observe that the sentence just before proves 'currit' to be right: 'Speed is not to be desired,' says Seneca, 'unless it can be checked at our pleasure,...and reduced from a run to a walk' (a *cursu* ad gradum reduci). Of previous scholars, the best-skilled in metre was Scaliger. Yet Scaliger's acquaintance with the metres of the *classical* age was by no means accurate; thus his anapæsts have the same fault as those of Buchanan and Grotius; and the iambic verses which he prefixed to his work *De Emendatione Temporum* have two metrical mistakes in four lines. While invariably mentioning Casaubon with the respect due to so great a name, Bentley has more than once occasion to indicate the false quantities which his conjectures involve. Thus a line of Sophocles, as given by Suidas, begins with the words πέπλους ('robes') τενίσαι. What is τενίσαι? Casaubon—followed by Meursius and by Gataker (one of the best English Hellenists before Bentley)— proposed κτενίσαι, 'to comb' or 'card.' Pointing out that this will not do, since the second syllable must be long, Bentley restores πέπλους τε νῆσαι, 'and to weave robes.'

As a commentator, he deals chiefly, though not exclusively, with points of grammar or metre bearing on the criticism of the text. Here he has two merits, each in a high degree; he instructs and suggests. The notes on Horace and Manilius, for example, constantly fail to persuade, but seldom fail to teach. It is to be wished that Bentley had written commentary, not merely in support of emendations, but continuously illustrating the language and matter of classical authors. If such a

commentary had been added to his critical notes on
Aristophanes, the whole must have been a great work.
His power in *general* commentary is best seen in his
treatment of particular points raised by his argument
on the Letters of Phalaris. Take, for instance, his
remarks on the sophist's use of πρόνοια to mean 'divine
Providence,' and of στοιχεῖον as 'a natural element;'
where he shows that, before Plato, the former was
used only of human forecast, and the latter to denote a
letter of the alphabet : or, again, his remark on such
phrases as λέγεται, 'it is said'—that Greek writers commonly use such phrases, not to intimate doubt, but, on the
contrary, where the literary witnesses are more numerous
than can conveniently be enumerated. Other comments
are of yet larger scope. Thus, speaking of the fact that
most ecclesiastical writers place the date of Pythagoras too
low, he notices the need of allowing for a general disturbing cause,—the tendency to represent Greek antiquity as
more recent than Jewish. Answering the objection that
a Greek comedy would not have admitted a glaring
anachronism, Bentley reminds Boyle that, in one of these
comedies, Hercules comes on the scene with his private
tutor, who gives him his choice of several standard works,
including Homer ; but the young hero chooses a treatise
on cookery which was popular in the dramatist's time.
Some of Bentley's happiest comments of this kind occur
in his reply to Anthony Collins, who in his 'Discourse of
Free-Thinking' had appealed to the most eminent of the
ancients. Here, for instance, is a remark on Cicero's
philosophical dialogues. ' In all the disputes he introduces between the various sects, after the speeches are
ended, every man sticks where he was before; not one con-
vert is made (as is common in modern dialogue), nor
brought over in the smallest article. For he avoided that

violation of decorum ; he had observed, in common life, that all persevered in their sects, and maintained every nostrum without reserve.'

Bentley's 'higher criticism'—of ancient history, chronology, philosophy, literature—is mainly represented by the dissertation on Phalaris : but his calibre can also be estimated by his sketchy treatment of particular topics in the reply to Collins and in the Boyle Lectures. Of the scholars before Bentley, Usher and Selden might be partly compared with him in this province; but the only one, perhaps, who had built similar work on a comparable basis of classical learning was Scaliger. In Bentley's estimation, to judge by the tone of his references to Scaliger, no one stood higher. With all the differences between Bentley and Scaliger, there was this essential resemblance, that both men vivified great masses of learning by ardent, though dissimilar, genius :

Spiritus intus alit, totamque infusa per artus
Mens agitat molem, et magno se in corpore miscet.

While Scaliger had constantly before him the conception of antiquity as a whole to be mentally grasped, Bentley's criticism rested on a knowledge more complete in detail; it was also conducted with a closer and more powerful logic. The fact which has told most against the popular diffusion of Bentley's fame is that he is so much greater than any one of his books. Probably many school-boys have passed through a stage of secretly wondering why so much was thought of this Bentley, known to them only as the proposer of some rash emendations on Horace. Bentley's true greatness is not easily understood until his work has been surveyed in its entirety, with a clear sense of the time at which it was done ; until the original learning and native power of his method are appreciated apart from the sometimes brilliant, sometimes

faulty result; until, in short, the letter of his record is lit
up for us by the living force of his character and mind.

What has been the nature of Bentley's influence on
the subsequent course of scholarship? In the first place it
cannot be properly said that he founded a school. That
phrase may express the relation of disciples to the master
who has personally formed them, as Ruhnken belongs to
the school of Hemsterhuys; or, where there has been no
personal intercourse, it may denote the tradition of a
well-defined scope or style; as the late Richard Shilleto
(in his masterly edition of Demosthenes 'On the Em-
bassy,' for instance) belongs to the school of Porson.
Wolf said that if Cambridge had required Bentley to
lecture on classics, he would probably have left a more
distinct impress on some of those who came after him.
Though the tone of Wolf's remark is more German than
English, it applies with peculiar point to Bentley, in
whom the scholar was before all things the man, and
who often writes like one who would have preferred to
speak. But neither thus, nor by set models of literary
achievement, did Bentley create anything so definite—or
so narrow—as a school. Goethe used the word 'daemonic'
to describe a power of mind over mind which eludes
natural analysis, but seems to involve a peculiar union of
keen insight with moral self-reliance. In the sphere of
scholarship, the influence which Bentley's spirit has exerted
through his writings might be called a great 'daemonic'
energy, a force which cannot be measured,—like that, for
instance, of Porson,—by the positive effect of particular
discoveries; a force which operates not only by the written
letter, but also, and more widely still, by suggestion, sti-
mulus, inspiration, almost as vivid as could be communi-
cated by the voice, the countenance, the apprehended
nature of a present teacher.

Bentley's influence has flowed in two main streams,—
the historical and literary criticism of classical antiquity,
as best seen in the dissertation on Phalaris ; the verbal
criticism, as seen in his work on classical texts. Holland,
and then Germany, received both currents. Wolf's inquiry into the origin of the Homeric poems, Niebuhr's
examination of Roman legends, are the efforts of a criticism to which Bentley's dissertation on Phalaris gave the
first pattern of method. On the other hand, Hermann's
estimate of Bentley's Terence is one of the earlier testimonies to the effect which Bentley's verbal criticism
had exercised ; and Professor Nettleship has told us that
the late Maurice Haupt, in his lectures at Berlin on
the Epistles of Horace, ranked Bentley second to no other
scholar. We, Bentley's countrymen, have felt his influence chiefly in the way of textual criticism. The historical and literary criticism by which he stimulated such
men as Wolf was comparatively unappreciated in England
until its effects returned upon this country from Germany.
Bunsen could justly say, 'historical philology is the discovery of Bentley,—the heritage and glory of German
learning.' At Cambridge, Bentley's home,—where Markland, Wasse, and John Taylor had known him personally,
—it was natural that the contemporary view of his merits
should be coloured by his own estimate; and he considered
verbal emendation as his own forte. This opinion prevailed in the Cambridge tradition, which from Markland
and Taylor passed into the school of Porson. It was
in vain that Richard Dawes disparaged Bentley's textual
criticism. Warburton and Lowth were more successful
in prejudicing English opinion against other aspects of
his work. That his labours on the Greek Testament were
so little known in England from his death to Lachmann's
time, is chiefly due to the fact (noticed by Tregelles) that

Bishop Marsh, in translating Michaelis, omitted the passage relating to Bentley. But while English recognition was thus limited, Holland honoured him by the mouths of Ruhnken and Valckenaer. And the memoir of Bentley by F. A. Wolf may be regarded as registering an estimate which Germany has not essentially altered.

The place of Bentley in literature primarily depends on the fact that he represents England among a few great scholars, of various countries, who helped to restore classical learning in Europe. Nor is he merely one among them; he is one with whom an epoch begins. Erasmus marks the highest point reached in the sixteenth century by the genial study of antiquity on its literary side. Scaliger expresses the effort, at once erudite and artistic, to comprehend antiquity as a whole in the light of verified history. Casaubon embodies the devoted endeavour to comprehend ancient society in the light of its recorded manners, without irradiating or disturbing the effect by any play of personal thought or feeling. With Bentley that large conception of antiquity on the 'real' side is still present, but as a condition tacitly presupposed, not as the evident guide of his immediate task. He feels the greatness of his predecessors as it could be felt only by their peer, but sees that the very foundations on which they built—the classical books themselves—must be rendered sound, if the edifice is to be upheld or completed. He does not disparage that 'higher' criticism in which his own powers were so signally proved; rather his object is to establish it firmly on the only basis which can securely support it, the basis of ascertained texts. His labours were fruitful both in Greek and in Latin. However we may estimate his felicity in the two languages respectively, it cannot be said that he gave to either a clear preference over the other.

This is distinctive of his position relatively to the general course of subsequent scholarship. During the latter part of the eighteenth century several causes conspired to fix attention upon Greek. The elastic freedom of the Greek language and literature, of Greek action and art, was congenial to the spirit of that time, insurgent as it was against traditional authority, and impatient to find a reasonable order of life by a return to nature. Wolf, in 1795, touched a chord which vibrated throughout Europe when he claimed the Iliad and the Odyssey as groups of songs which in a primitive age had spoken directly to the hearts of the people. His theory, raising a host of special questions, stimulated research in the whole range of that matchless literature which begins with Homer. The field of Greek studies, as compared with Latin, was still comparatively fresh. Latin had long been familiar as the language which scholars wrote, or even spoke; and the further progress of Latin learning was delayed by the belief that there was little more to learn. Greek, on the other hand, attracted acute minds not only by its intrinsic charm, but by the hope of discovery; the Greek scholar, like the Greek sailor of old, was attended by visions of treasures that might await him in the region of the sunset.

Porson was born in 1759 and died in 1808. In his life-time, and for more than a generation after his death, scholars were principally occupied with Greek. Among many eminent names, it would be enough to mention Wyttenbach, Brunck, Hermann, Boeckh, Lobeck, Bekker, Elmsley, Dobree, Blomfield, Gaisford, Thirlwall. In Latin scholarship, Heyne's Virgil was perhaps the most considerable performance of Porson's day. Then Niebuhr arose, and turned new currents of interest towards Rome. His examination of early Roman tradition did much the

same work for Latin which Wolf's Homeric theory had
done for Greek. Ideas of startling novelty stimulated
the critical study of a whole literature ; and the value of
the impulse was independent of the extent to which the
ideas themselves were sound. Niebuhr's thoughts, like
Wolf's, were given to the world in a propitious hour.
Wolf broached views welcome to the mind of the
Revolution ; Niebuhr proposed a complex problem of
fascinating interest at a moment when intellectual
pursuits were resumed with a new zest after the exhaustion
of the Napoleonic wars. And then, at no long interval,
came the works which may be regarded as fundamental
in the recent Latin philology,—those of Lachmann,
Ritschl, Mommsen.

Bentley's name is the last of first-rate magnitude
which occurs above the point at which Greek and Latin
studies begin to diverge. His critical method, his
pregnant ideas have influenced the leaders of progress
in both fields. Wolf's memoir of Bentley has been
mentioned. Niebuhr also speaks of him as towering like
a giant amid a generation of dwarfs. His genius was
recognised by Ritschl as by Porson. It is still possible
to ask, Was Bentley stronger in Greek or in Latin? I
have heard a very eminent scholar say,—in Latin : the
general voice would probably say,—in Greek : and this is
hardly disputable, if our test is to be success in textual
criticism. Bentley has given few, if any, Latin emendations so good as his best on Aristophanes, Callimachus,
Nicander and some other Greek authors. Yet the
statement needs to be guarded and explained. In
Bentley's time, Latin studies were more advanced than
Greek. Bentley's emendations, as a general rule, are best
when the text is worst. The Greek texts, in which the
first harvest had not yet been reaped, offered him a

better field than the Latin. His personal genius, with
its vivacity somewhat impatient of formula, was also
more Greek than Latin; his treatment of Greek usually
seems more sympathetic; but it might be doubted
whether his positive knowledge of the Latin language
and literature was inferior. If it is said that there are
flaws in his Latin prose, it may be replied that we have
none of his Greek prose.

The gain of scholarship during the last fifty years
has been chiefly in three provinces,—study of manuscripts, study of inscriptions, and comparative philology.
The direct importance of archæology for classical learning has of late years been winning fuller recognition—
to the advantage of both. In Bentley's time no one of
these four studies had yet become scientific. That very
fact best illustrates the calibre of the man who, a century
and a half ago, put forth principles of textual criticism
afterwards adopted by Lachmann; merited the title,
'first of critics,' from such an editor of Greek inscriptions
as Boeckh; divined the presence of the digamma in the
text of Homer; treated an obscure branch of numis-
matics with an insight which the most recent researches,
aided by new resources, recognise as extraordinary.
Bentley's qualities, mental and moral, fitted him to be a
pioneer over a wide region, rather than, like Porson, the
perfect cultivator of a limited domain; Bentley cleared
new ground, made new paths, opened new perspectives,
ranged through the length and breadth of ancient literature as Hercules, in the *Trachiniae* of Sophocles, claims
to have roamed through Hellas, sweeping from hill, lake
and forest those monstrous forms before which superstition
had quailed, or which helpless apathy had suffered to
infest the dark places of the land.

Probably the study of classical antiquity, in the

largest sense, has never been more really vigorous than it
is at the present day.   If so, it is partly because that
study relies no longer upon a narrow or exclusive pre-
scription, but upon a reasonable perception of its proper
place among the studies which belong to a liberal
education; and because the diffusion of that which is
specially named science has at the same time spread abroad
the only spirit in which any kind of knowledge can be
prosecuted to a result of lasting intellectual value.   While
every year tends to refine the subdivision of labour in
that vast field, Bentley's work teaches a simple lesson
which is still applicable to every part of it.   The literary
activity of the present day has multiplied attractive
facilities for becoming acquainted with the ancient classics
at second hand.   Every sensible person will rejoice
that such facilities exist;   they are excellent in their
own way.   Only it is important not to forget the
difference between the knowledge at second hand and
the knowledge at first hand, whether regard is had to
the educational effect of the process, or to the worth of
the acquisition, or to the hope of further advance.   Even
with a Bentley's power, a Bentley could have been made
only by his method,—by his devoted and systematic
study, not of books about the classics, but of the classical
texts themselves; by testing, at each step, his comprehension of what he read ; by not allowing the mere
authority of tradition to supersede the free exercise of
independent judgment ; and by always remembering that
the very right of such judgment to independence must
rest on the patience, the intelligence, the completeness
with which the tradition itself has been surveyed.

For EU product safety concerns, contact us at Calle de José Abascal, 56–1°,
28003 Madrid, Spain or eugpsr@cambridge.org.

www.ingramcontent.com/pod-product-compliance
Ingram Content Group UK Ltd.
Pitfield, Milton Keynes, MK11 3LW, UK
UKHW010338140625
459647UK00010B/685